BODY
SIGNS

BABY SIGNS

*How to talk with your baby
before your baby can talk*

LINDA ACREDOLO, PH.D
AND SUSAN GOODWYN, PH.D.

Vermilion
LONDON

Text © Susan Goodwyn and Linda Acredolo 2000
Cover photograph © Don Mason/The Stock Market 1992

This edition first published in the United Kingdom
in 2000 by Vermilion,
an imprint of Ebury Press
Random House, 20 Vauxhall Bridge Road, London SW1V 2SA

The Random House Group Limited Reg. No. 954009

www.randomhouse.co.uk

A CIP catalogue record for this book is available from
the British Library.

Illustrations in Chapter 10 by Steve Gillig

ISBN 9780091851682

The Random House Group Limited supports The Forest Stewardship Council® (FSC®), the leading international forest-certification organisation. Our books carrying the FSC label are printed on FSC®-certified paper. FSC is the only forest-certification scheme supported by the leading environmental organisations, including Greenpeace. Our paper procurement policy can be found at www.randomhouse.co.uk/environment

MIX
Paper from
responsible sources
FSC
www.fsc.org   FSC® C016897

Printed and bound in Great Britain by Clays Ltd, St Ives plc

This book is dedicated to
Kate, who first opened our eyes to Baby Signs;
and to Kai, Brandon and Leanne,
who followed in her footsteps,
Baby Signing their own way into our homes
and into our hearts.

Contents

Acknowledgements

A bove all, we would like to thank the many families, including parents and children, who have participated in our research studies and workshops over the years. Without their untiring and creative Baby Sign efforts and their willingness to share their time and their stories, our knowledge of the advantages of Baby Signs would not be what it is today. We are especially indebted to those who have allowed us to include photographs of their beautiful children in this book.

Our deep appreciation also goes to the students, numbering over a hundred by now, who have worked long hours in our labs helping us to evaluate the benefits of Baby Signs in order that we might share them with you. While it is impossible to acknowledge every student individually, we would like to express our special appreciation to Lynn Arner-Cross, Amy Fulmer, Jeannie Lee, Carla Andalis, Aimee Sullivan, Brenda Baxter, Terry Wilson, Teri Ouimet, Joyce Humphrey and Cathy Brown, who were the mainstays of the Baby Sign Project in its first few years. We are also indebted to the National Institute of Child Health and Human Development for the research grant, without which the longitudinal study of the effects of Baby Signs would not have been possible.

Most of what we know about the benefits of Baby Signs in day-care settings is due to the continuous efforts of Kathleen Grey, Director of the Infant Program at the Child and Family Studies Center, University of California, Davis. Kathleen's enthusiasm for our work was spontaneous and truly inspirational. Her frequent reminders that Baby Signs have an important role to play within the carer-infant relationship were particularly helpful, often providing just the morale boost we needed to get through difficult times. In addition to Kathleen, we are also indebted to her assistant, Pauline Wooliever, who carried out much of the day-to-day labour involved in the Center's Baby Sign Project and to whom we could always turn for both insights and information. Of course, all of Kathleen and Pauline's efforts would have come to naught without the enthusiastic involvement of the families with infants enrolled in the Center. These infants have provided the clearest evidence yet that Baby Signs can, and should, be part of every day-care curriculum.

Our gratitude also goes to Betsy Amster, our literary agent, who helped us shape our ideas and our writing. Her faith in what we were doing was unwavering, and her valuable suggestions, skilful editing and good-natured humour kept us focused throughout the process.

A special note of thanks goes to our partners, Larry and Peter, who have stuck with us through thick and thin. None of this would have been possible without their patience, enthusiasm, love and support. Some weeks it probably seemed that we spent more time with each other than we did with them. And they were right!

Last but not least, we would like to say thanks to the staff and all the other good folks at Café Roma where the ideas for this book were born and brought to fruition. We appreciate their patience when we hogged the tables and their tolerance of our Baby Sign antics. Now they'll know what we've been doing these past ten years!

CHAPTER ONE

Introducing Baby Signs

Even though she is too young to say more than a very few words, thirteen-month-old Jennifer loves books. As her dad, Mark, settles on the sofa after dinner, she toddles over. Holding her palms together facing up, she opens and closes them. Mark's immediate, "Oh, OK. Let's get a book to read," satisfies her, and she soon returns with her favourite animal book, cuddles up close and begins turning the pages.

With delight she looks at a picture, scrapes her fingers across her chest, and looks up with a broad smile at Mark. "Yes, you're right! That's a zebra!" Mark says, answering her grin with one of his own.

The next page brings Jennifer's fingertip to her nose with an up-down motion and a proud "Yes, that's an elephant!" from Mark. As the pages turn, Jennifer bounces her torso up and down, opens her mouth wide, tilting her head back and rubs her hands together. Without hesitation Mark acknowledges that in each case she is right again: that is a kangaroo, that is a hippopotamus, and that is water the hippo is swimming in. They continue through the book, pride clearly showing in both their eyes.

Almost anything that interests your baby is a candidate for a Baby Sign. All you need is a simple body motion and a receptive audience. Here, eighteen-month-old Leanne is caught in mid-sign, bouncing her torso up and down to tell us she has just seen a kangaroo during an outing to the zoo.

Let's take a close look at what just happened here: thirteen-month-old Jennifer *told* her father what was in the book, and her father understood. Yet she used absolutely no words, at least in the conventional sense. Instead, Jennifer was using easy non-verbal gestures – Baby Signs – that she and her dad had agreed would stand for *zebra, elephant, kangaroo* and the other things she wanted to bring to her father's attention. With Baby Signs in her repertoire, Jennifer could enjoy interactions with her father that otherwise would have to wait until she could talk. And considering how slowly babies learn even easy words like *ball* and *doggy*, let alone words like *kangaroo* and *zebra*, there is no doubt that the result of waiting would be months and months of wasted time.

It doesn't matter how big or little you are, successful communication with other people makes life better. In fact, for the young and helpless it may be even more important.

> *Andrew, fourteen months old, wakes up in a fright, wailing loudly for Laura, his mum. As she stumbles into his room asking, "What's the matter, sweetie? Don't you feel well?" Andrew furiously pats his chest. "Oh, you're scared!" answers Laura, as she swoops him up out of his cot and hugs him close. "What is it, darling? Did you have a bad dream?" she asks. Andrew's response is to pat his nose repeatedly, looking with wide eyes at his mother. "Oh. It's that clown that Grandma brought. You don't like it so close at night. That's OK, sweetie. Let's take it away for tonight so you can get back to sleep." As Laura settles him back down in his cot, Andrew moves his thumb to his lips, tipping it up and down. "And you want a drink? OK, I'll be right back with some water."*
>
> *After removing the clown, delivering the water and giving him one last kiss, Laura returns to her own bed, the crisis quickly and successfully resolved.*

Consider again what young Jennifer and Andrew have in common. The answer is successful communication. In each case a baby, even without words, was able to convey a message and to enjoy the experience of being

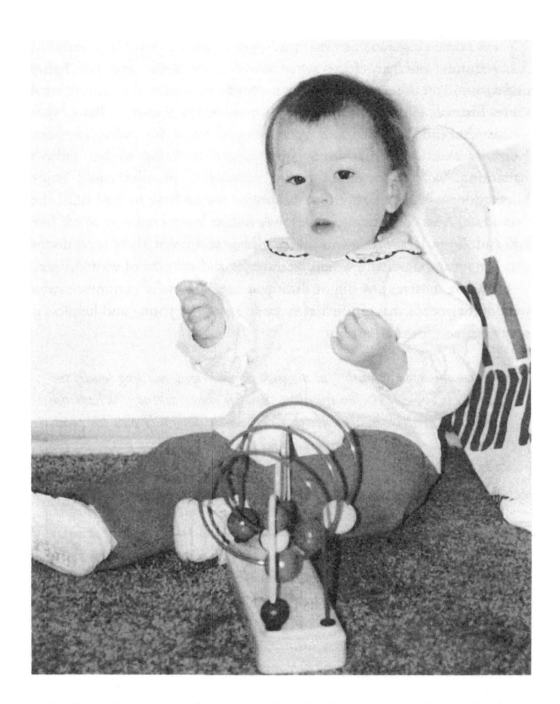

Baby Signs for favourite foods, as well as for favourite animals, tend to be popular among babies. Here, twelve-month-old Maya demonstrates the simple finger-pinching gesture that many of our parents and carers use to mean "cereal".

quickly and accurately understood. Interchanges such as these foster feelings of competence and help avoid frustration. Unlike many babies at these ages, Jennifer and Andrew weren't totally dependent on pointing, crying or an urgent "Uh uh uh!" to get a message across. And contrary to what some people may think, their Baby Sign experiences in no way discouraged them from learning to talk. In fact, their experiences had just the opposite effect, providing Jennifer and Andrew with exactly the kind of rich, interpersonal conversation that yields *faster* rather than slower language development.

These two real-life examples of Baby Signs in action also illustrate how much smarter babies are than we often assume. Jennifer and Andrew may not be talking yet, but that doesn't mean they aren't thinking. They know quite well what *they* want to "say", and with Baby Signs they can say it. At the same time, those around them get a wonderful glimpse into just how much is going on in their heads. Jennifer has demonstrated an impressive grasp of the animal kingdom and Andrew has revealed an ability that even many adults envy: the ability to label his emotions. Unlike most parents, who have to guess what their babies are thinking, Jennifer's father and Andrew's mother can easily follow their children's lead, focusing attention where the *babies* most need it to be. What parent wouldn't welcome such a window into his or her baby's mind?

The Goal of This Book

With this book, we want to help you and your baby learn to take advantage of Baby Signs such as these. Just as Jennifer and Andrew have done, your baby can easily learn simple gestures for objects, events and needs. With these signs literally at your baby's fingertips, communication between you can flourish during that difficult time from about nine to thirty months, when your baby's desire to communicate outstrips her capacity to say words. By increasing the number of gestures in your baby's repertoire, the two of you can "talk" about a lot more things than your baby's few early words would permit.

But the benefits don't stop there. Our ten years of scholarly research on Baby Signs have proved conclusively that adding these gestures to a

Thirteen-month-old Tristan points with one index finger at the hog while using his other index finger to press his nose, his Baby Sign for "pig". The county show was much more fun for everyone once he could "talk" about the animals himself.

baby's repertoire not only leads to better communication; it also speeds up the process of learning to talk, stimulates intellectual development, enhances self-esteem, and strengthens the bond between parent and infant. Parents wanting to get their baby off to a good start simply can't go wrong with Baby Signs.

And why are we so sure your baby can do it? The answer is simple: in a lifetime of observing babies, as well as a decade of research on Baby Signs, we haven't yet met a baby who couldn't – and neither have you! Without a second thought, all parents teach their babies to wave a hand for *bye-bye* when someone leaves and to shake their heads back and forth for *no* and up and down for *yes*. Think about it. These are Baby Signs. Just like Jennifer's *kangaroo* motion or Andrew's sign for *drink*, each is a simple gesture with a specific meaning, consciously or unconsciously modelled for infants by their parents. In their eagerness to join the social world around them, babies pick up *bye-bye, yes* and *no* gestures easily, often months before the corresponding words come in.

All too often, however, parents stop there, never realising their infant's full Baby Sign potential. With this book you will learn how easy it is to take this natural tendency a step further and open up an exciting channel of communication between you and your child. *Bye-bye* may be the first sign your baby learns, but it certainly need not be the last.

Our Own Introduction to Baby Signs

Over the past ten years we have introduced hundreds of parents, teachers and paediatricians to the advantages of Baby Signs. Invariably the response is amazement at the simplicity of what we are advocating, and enthusiasm for the benefits we describe. But where did our own enthusiasm come from? Who convinced *us* that Baby Signs were indeed something special? How we happened upon the phenomenon of Baby Signs and why we believe so strongly in our message is a story in itself.

It all began in a personal way when one of us (Linda) gave birth to a baby daughter, Kate. At the time, we were both busy university lecturers and doing research on older children, with only a passing interest in how babies learn to talk. All that changed, however, when baby Kate reached

A hot summer's day at the zoo was the occasion for this picture. Thirteen-month-old Kate is telling her mum, and the camera, about the kangaroo in the enclosure behind her. It was the first real kangaroo she had ever seen.

twelve months old and three events occurred. See if you can guess, as we had to, how Kate came up with the ideas for the Baby Signs she spontaneously invented.

Event 1: Kate and Linda were in the doctor's surgery, where a large aquarium was provided to keep patients entertained. Kate ran to the tank, pointed excitedly and made a blowing gesture – whff whff whff – as if she were blowing out a candle. Until she learned to say "fish" at nineteen months, this blowing gesture worked perfectly well as Kate's "word" for any fish that came her way.

Event 2: Kate and Linda were out in the garden. Kate pointed at a rose, looked at Linda and sniffed repeatedly. From then on until the word for flower arrived at twenty months, a sniffing gesture was her "word" for real flowers, pictures of flowers, toy flowers – any flowers she needed to "talk" about.

Event 3: While in Linda's office, Kate saw a daddy-long-legs in the corner. Grabbing Linda's hand, she pointed to it and rubbed her index fingers together in a gesture she clearly intended as a label. With this "word" at her command, she became enchanted with looking for spiders everywhere, from the tiniest baby spider in the house to the tarantula at the zoo.

These were only the first of Kate's Baby Signs. But because they came out of the blue, we found ourselves scrambling to catch up with Kate. Where had these three signs come from? We soon figured out that each one had grown directly out of a specific game Kate played with her favourite people. Take the *flower* sign. As many babies do, Kate had long enjoyed a routine in which her parents would sniff a flower themselves and then thrust it under her nose for her to do the same, all the while saying things like "See the flower, Kate! Pretty flower!" Clearly, Kate remembered the connection between the action and the object, and she trusted that her parents would too.

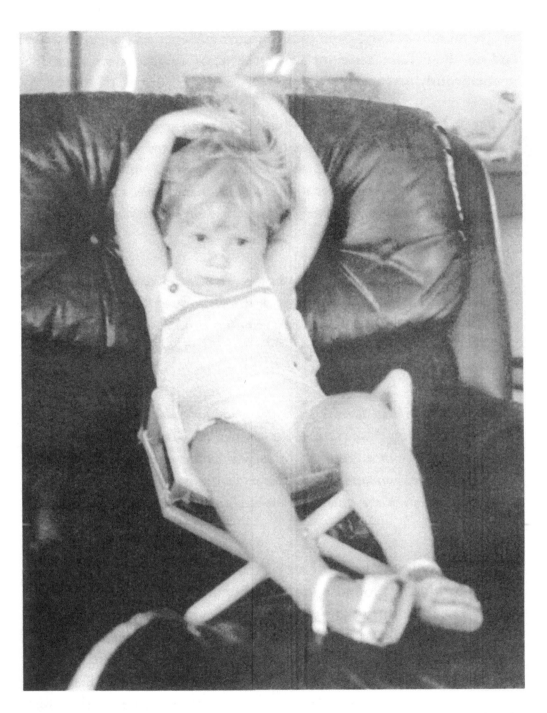

Mesmerised by Sesame Street, *fourteen-month-old Kate identifies "Big Bird" with a hands-over-head Baby Sign. She also had Baby Signs for "Kermit" and "Cookie Monster".*

The same was true for the *spider* sign. As part of the "Eency Weency Spider" song, Kate had learned to rub her fingers together as her version of the *spider* going "up the waterspout". In her eagerness to talk about the world around her, Kate once again borrowed an action, this time an action that people had specifically tried to get her to learn as part of that nursery song. She learned it all right, but then went well beyond the song itself by using the same action to talk about the world of real spiders.

It was a little more difficult for us to figure out where Kate had come across a blowing action for *fish*. She hadn't seen many real fish in her short life and the family didn't even eat fish. The answer became clear at bedtime. As a baby gift for Kate, a student of Linda's had made a lovely mobile to hang over her crib – and, yes, you guessed it – the mobile was composed of delicately intertwined ribbon fish. "See the fish! See the fishies swim," Linda would say each night as Linda and Kate took turns blowing on the mobile. This well-established bedtime ritual was all Kate needed to help her "talk" about fish of every kind.

Once we figured out what Kate was trying to do, we decided to help her along. It was so easy! We simply looked for actions to pair with objects she liked: wiggling a finger for *caterpillar*, opening our mouths wide for *hippo*, putting a palm over our mouths for *Cookie Monster*, waving a hand back and forth when things were hot, and on and on. She learned these Baby Signs eagerly and used them with the same joy she had when expressing *fish*, *spider* and *flower*. None of this, we were interested to see, stopped her from learning real words too. In her enthusiasm for communicating, she used *whatever* means she could. It wasn't long before she had forty-eight words plus twenty-eight Baby Signs in her repertoire. She was quite the conversationalist!

Finally, as we now know happens with all babies, the words started coming so easily that they simply took over. Although it was sad in a way to see the signs go, it was very exciting to see Kate's language skills continue to blossom. Kate's use of Baby Signs had clearly got her off to a good start. Of equal importance, the whole experience left us eager to see if other infants were using them too.

Many other songs and rhymes besides "The Eency Weency Spider" have actions that can become Baby Signs. Here, thirteen-month-old Kate contributes her moon Baby Sign (circling palm) to "I See the Moon and the Moon Sees Me". She also took great pleasure in using this sign while reading the classic bedtime book Goodnight Moon.

Wearing long white ears of her own, nineteen-month-old Kate uses her finger gesture for "bunny" (alternating bent and straight) to tell someone that a bunny is indeed what she is supposed to be.

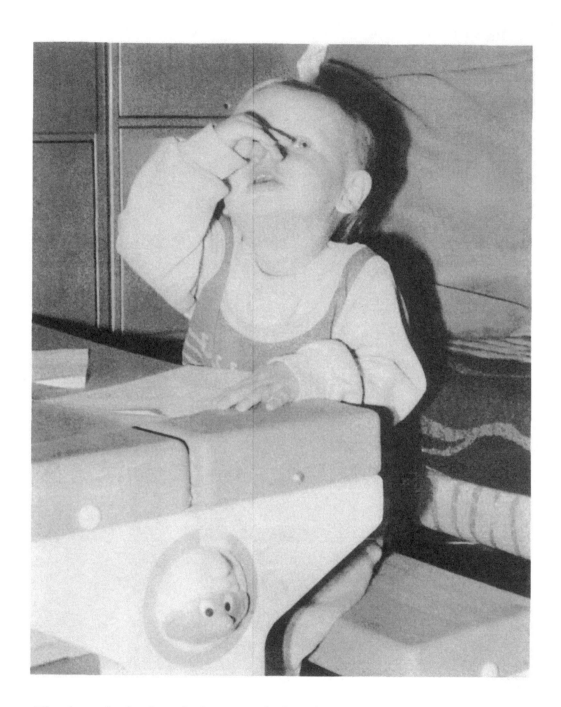

There's no doubt that elephants, with their long trunks and big ears, hold a special fascination for babies. Here, fourteen-month-old Kai labels an elephant picture. He also routinely used this Baby Sign to talk about real elephants, toy elephants and his favourite elephant-covered sweatshirt.

Out of Our Sitting Room, into the Laboratory

Our first step was systematically to begin interviewing parents to find out whether Kate was unique or babies routinely use Baby Signs. Within days of starting our interviews, the answer was clear. Not only did many parents give us examples of signs their babies were using, but the babies themselves would occasionally interrupt our visit to "talk" to mum, including a sign or two in the process. Seventeen-month-old Elizabeth was one of the first:

> We had just nicely settled down in the kitchen with Peg, Elizabeth's mum, when across the floor and under our feet came a colourful, clockwork elephant. Startled, we watched as the elephant disappeared beside the fridge. A few minutes later two high-energy playmates – Elizabeth and the family dog – burst into the kitchen. Although we didn't immediately connect the two events, it turned out toddler and puppy were after the toy. But where was it? Neither Elizabeth nor the dog had a clue. What Elizabeth did have, however, was the capacity to ask for her mother's help. Within seconds, Elizabeth caught her mother's eye and raised an index finger to her nose, moving it up and down in a clear imitation of an elephant's trunk. "Oh, the elephant!" Peg answered. "It's over there next to the fridge. Let me help you get it."

Although Peg and Elizabeth treated this event as routine, we were genuinely excited. Here, right before our eyes, was a true Baby Sign in action. As Kate had done with her signs, Elizabeth had learned the *elephant* sign from her parents' playful use of the gesture in games and routines. Elizabeth took her cue from them, successfully adopting the *elephant* sign to label pictures, toys and even once the vacuum cleaner with its long, trunk-like hose. Much to our delight, the story didn't end there. A few weeks later we received a phone call from Peg: Elizabeth was now trying to say the word *elephant* and using the gesture to help her parents understand what "e-fnt" was intended to mean!

We learned a great deal from families like Elizabeth's, and the more we learned, the more convinced we became that Baby Signs are not an unusual addition to family life. Almost all babies seem to develop at least a few signs beyond the universal *bye-bye*, *yes*, and *no*, usually sometime between nine and twenty-four months. We also noticed that some babies take to the idea with particular enthusiasm, creating an impressive variety of signs for favourite objects and important needs. Invariably, these babies had families who shared their enthusiasm and encouraged the gesturing. Moreover, it tended to be the case that the more Baby Signs an infant used, the *faster* that child learned to talk. This was our best clue yet about the effect of Baby Signs on vocal language development. The Baby Signs seemed, if anything, to speed up the process.

In the years since that first interview study, we have confirmed that Baby Signs help children's development. In a large-scale experiment funded by the National Institute for Child Health and Human Development in America, we studied 140 families with eleven-month-old babies for two years. One-third of these families were encouraged to use Baby Signs; the other two-thirds were not. Our plan was to compare the groups periodically to see if the Baby Sign experience was having any effects – good, bad or indifferent.

So what did we find? In a nutshell, we found only positive effects on the Baby Sign babies, who outperformed the other babies in comparison after comparison. They scored higher in intelligence tests, understood more words, had larger vocabularies and engaged in more sophisticated play. Most gratifying of all, however, were the ways in which parents described the experience of using Baby Signs. They talked enthusiastically about advantages we were expecting: increased communication, decreased frustration and an enriched parent-infant bond. However, they also alerted us to many more subtle advantages we hadn't considered, like increased self-confidence and interest in books.

"Frankly, we were worried at first about trying it with Lori because it seemed in a way to be the opposite of teaching her to talk. And I really wanted to talk to her! But as soon as she began to catch on – the fish gesture was the first one – it was like opening a floodgate. Like she'd been waiting for some way to let me know what was going on inside

her head. Suddenly it was fish here, fish there, fish everywhere – even the frozen ones at the supermarket. It was the same with each sign she learned. In fact, I ended up enjoying the signs so much that I was almost sad to see the words come in and the signs go out. But it was great fun while it lasted, and I bet we'll never see the end of the head start it gave her."

– Parent participant in the Baby Signs experiment

Helping Your Own Baby Talk About the World

Infancy is a time of revelling in the wonders of the world, of discovering how things work, and of sharing with important people the joys and fears that fill each day. Babies are as curious as cats but (fortunately) much more social. They are not satisfied with simply noticing the aeroplane in the sky, the bird on the window sill, or the flowers in the garden; they want to *tell* someone about them. In fact, as Penelope Leach points out in her successful parenting book *Babyhood*, the primary motivation spurring babies towards language is the chance it provides to socialise with others: "The first words … are almost always used in the context of calling the adult's attention to something, inviting her to share the experiences" (p. 273).

How sad it is, Leach laments, that so many people view babies as uninterested in language and uninteresting to talk to, simply because the babies cannot yet say much themselves. Such attitudes all too often mean missed opportunities to foster language and, perhaps even more important, to strengthen the bond between parent and child so critical to healthy development. In *Your Growing Child* (pp. 442–443), Leach recommends a more helpful approach:

"What can I do to help my child acquire and use language well?" The biggest single step is a negative one: to get rid of the common notion that language means talking; that talking means using words and that therefore the whole process of language-learning is delayed until a baby

is nearly a year old. Language is communication between one person and another ... So if you wait to interest yourself in your child's language until she can speak, you will have missed a great deal of the fun.

What we propose to you in this book is how to take full advantage of your baby's hidden talents. Babies *can* communicate if only we will let them. And the rewards are sweet. By adding Baby Signs to his fledgling attempts to talk, your baby can reach out to others, have his horizons expanded and, best of all, forge bonds of affection and satisfaction with you that can last a lifetime.

CHAPTER TWO

Where Baby Signs Fit in the Jigsaw Puzzle of Language

How can Baby Signs accomplish so much? To understand their usefulness fully, you need to take Penelope Leach's advice and get rid of the idea that learning language just means learning how to talk. Once you do that, it's much easier to understand the different developmental tasks your baby has to conquer in the exciting journey towards language.

When we describe the development of language to parents and students, we suggest that they think of it as similar to putting together the pieces of a jigsaw puzzle. Language, like a puzzle picture, requires the contribution of many unique pieces. When constructing a jigsaw puzzle, you may put many pieces in place without the nature of the picture being revealed. And then you place a central piece. Suddenly, as it joins with the other pieces, a distinctive part of the

Although babies most often use the sign for "more" to request food, in this case eighteen-month-old Brandon uses it to ask his mother to take another picture.

picture emerges. It is the placement of that critical piece that allows the other pieces to reflect themselves – to define their contribution to the larger picture.

The same is true for language development. As a child develops, many "pieces" fall into place one by one. The piece we are most familiar with, of course, is speech – that is, the ability to combine sounds to form actual words. Because many people mistakenly think of speech as the sum total of what language is, they are surprised to learn that speech itself is a relatively late addition to the picture. The irony is that until children are able to speak words – until the critical speech piece is in place – we are often unaware of important advances they have already made.

One advantage of Baby Signs is that they enable your baby to show you, even before he talks, just how much of the puzzle he's already worked out. Let's take a brief look at these underlying accomplishments and how they develop.

Sound Play

When a baby finally produces a true word, she is demonstrating an impressive degree of mastery over all the large and small body parts necessary to make the particular sounds involved. There's the tongue to place, the lips to form, the nasal passages to shape, the vocal cords to control, the breathing to regulate, and much more. Grown-ups find this all so easy that they frequently don't realise what a daunting task it represents. Indeed, this complexity poses such an obstacle to communicating that it motivates babies to use Baby Signs. Baby Signs allow babies temporarily to bypass the sound system and get on with the important business of communication.

Eventually, however, they do conquer the sound system. How does this happen? Given the complexities involved, it's not surprising that babies begin the process very early. Long before they are able to say words, they practise the sounds of language. Starting with vowel sounds at around three months and adding consonant sounds around six months, they begin to babble away, often sounding so conversational that you are sure your baby is telling you something important. If only you could translate! But before twelve months, these sounds are rarely

Twelve-month-old Karen uses a Baby Sign for "frog", sticking her tongue in and out, to talk about her favourite Muppet, Kermit.

meaningful words. They constitute, quite simply, vocal play. Such play teaches your baby important lessons about how his mouth works. What he is learning is an essential piece of the puzzle. Finally, around his first birthday, one or two true words may appear on the scene. It's an exciting beginning but also an exciting endpoint to the months of rehearsal leading up to the big event.

Learning to Relate

Another puzzle piece that has already developed by the time the first words appear is social skill: the ability to relate to people. If you think about it, you can easily see that language is first and foremost a social activity. We primarily use language to get our needs met, to relate to other people, to feel connected and to share our experiences.

Social relations develop very easily and very early in a baby's life, although this might not be readily apparent to you. But think about your baby's very first smiles. Although these clearly looked like smiles to you, you weren't quite sure what your baby was smiling about. Your friends and relatives probably told you, "It's only wind!" But then, when your baby was around four to six weeks old, it was perfectly clear – she was smiling at you! Your baby was displaying what is known as the "social smile", a smile that is a response to another human being and an indication of the beginning of a social relationship.

The feeling of excitement that parents experience when they see their baby's first social smile is indescribable. It is as if their baby has just said "hello" for the first time. Parents recognise that their baby has taken a major step towards becoming an active partner in their social relations. And it is through these early social interactions that babies develop their desire to communicate and their motivation to master the necessary skills.

Learning to Get a Message Across

A third piece of the puzzle is the ability to engage in intentional communication. What we mean by this phrase is the ability to try through purposeful action to get a message across to someone else. It may surprise you to learn that this piece of the puzzle takes quite a while to develop.

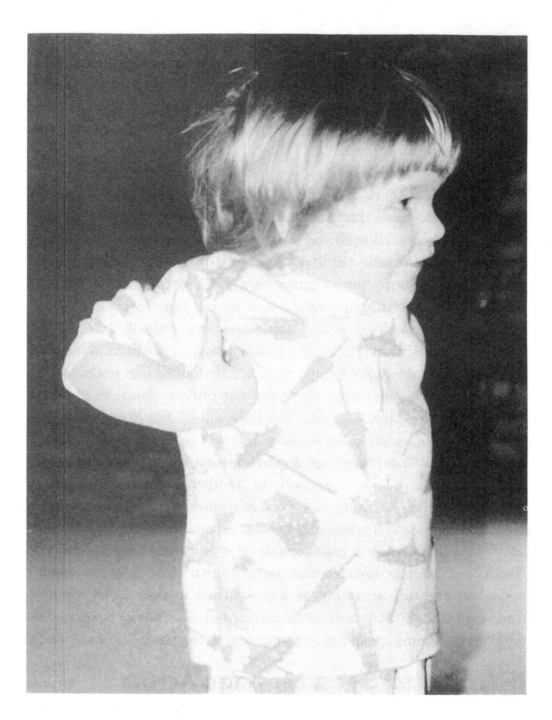

Baby Signs work in part because they are so much fun to do and so much fun to watch. Take the monkey sign modelled here. Could you resist such a performance?

Although babies are clearly communicating from the time they are born, they aren't aware that they are doing so until relatively late in the first year. Fortunately for them, parents respond to their needs anyway.

Early signals, even though they are not intentional, are actually quite interesting in and of themselves. Crying is by far the most obvious. Already during the first few weeks, young babies' cries begin to sound different depending on the source of their discomfort. Research has demonstrated what parents have long known: when a baby is in pain, his cry sounds different from when he is hungry, or bored. Although he is not intentionally communicating this distinction to his mother, she is clearly receiving a message about his feelings and is able to respond appropriately. If her baby's cry sounds as if he is in pain, she rushes to his aid. If his cry indicates that he's hungry, she may quickly finish what she is doing before she goes in to nurse him. Or if it sounds as if he is bored, she may simply begin to talk to him from a distance. Unaware that any message is being conveyed, he cries simply as a natural reaction to his internal bodily state.

Language, in contrast, is defined by *intentional* communication. How do you know when a baby's communications are intentional? Picture this very common behaviour in young babies. The baby reaches for a toy that is well beyond her reach. She looks at her dad and then back to the toy. Her behaviour is purposeful. Her intention is to get Dad to hand her the toy. And if Dad notices this behaviour, she is likely to succeed. The development of intention allows a baby to use even her most fledgling communication skills as a means to an end. She can now do something to produce desired and predictable results, an essential function of language.

Forming Concepts

Mastering intentional communication is just one more piece in the puzzle of language. Babies also must learn what things there are in the world to communicate *about*. Take, for example, the challenge of learning the apparently simple concepts of "dog" and "cat." From our grown-up perspective, this hardly seems difficult: dogs bark, cats meow;

Parents are often surprised to realize how attentive babies are to the sights and sounds around them. Sixteen-month-old Turner is no exception. Using his Baby Sign for "noise", he lets his child-minder know he hears the ringing of a telephone.

dogs nibble frantically at their bellies, cats leisurely lick; dogs act like clowns, cats have dignity. These are at least some of the salient differences that babies gradually learn to appreciate. But that's only half of the challenge of developing a concept like "dog". Every baby also has to learn what it is that a chihuahua and a collie, or a poodle and a dachshund, share that qualifies them all to be called dogs. After all, in some ways a chihuahua would seem to have more in common with the family cat than with an alsatian. But babies do figure it out. They learn not only about dogs and cats, but about everything else from apples to zebras.

Exactly how they accomplish all this so fast remains one of the most intriguing mysteries in all of language development. What we do know is that babies are incredibly busy gathering information and constantly refining their concepts. It is quite common for young babies to think that horses, cows and sheep are all "doggies" and that all men are "Daddy". This clearly indicates that they are forming some basic concepts – a "doggy" is something with four legs and a tail, and a "Daddy" is any grown-up man. With more and more experience, babies gradually clarify their concepts so that they come to understand that dogs are dogs, cows are cows, and Daddy is only that one special man who tickles their tummy and tucks them into bed at night. As children become able to form basic concepts, another critical piece of the language puzzle moves into place. For babies to use words correctly, they must first understand what concepts these words are meant to represent.

Using Symbols

Once babies begin to understand that words represent concepts, yet another puzzle piece has been added to the language picture: the ability to use symbols. What are symbols, and how do babies develop an appreciation for their power? A symbol is something that can stand for or represent something else. For example, a £5 note is a symbol. Objectively, it is just a piece of paper that has little inherent worth. However, the British have agreed that a fiver represents a proportion of our country's wealth. Because of this agreement, the note has symbolic value. Language also is symbolic. That is, words are just sounds that represent concepts we

In the park with his Baby Sign forerunner, Kate, twelve-month-old Brandon tells his mum, Lisa, that he hears an aeroplane (one arm up) overhead. Notice Brandon's eye contact with Lisa, a sure sign of intentional communication.

want to talk about. For example, if you want to communicate to your children that you're leaving to go to work, you are likely to say "Good-bye", or, "See you later". These sounds represent the message that you intend to convey.

The ability to use symbols develops gradually over the first year of a baby's life. When a baby motors a wooden block across the floor or feeds her teddy bear with a stick, she is demonstrating her symbolic ability. In each case she is using a symbol – the block as a symbol to represent a car and the stick as a symbol to represent a spoon. By the beginning of her second year, she will also begin to use language symbols. She will eagerly attend to the sounds of speech she hears around her and recruit them as symbols to represent her developing concepts.

Signs as Symbols

Although your baby's first words are clear evidence of the development of language, it is important, for the purpose of understanding the role of Baby Signs, to know that language symbols are not limited to words. When leaving for work, you could just as easily wave your hand as say, "Good-bye", and your children still would understand your intended message. Non-verbal gestures, such as waving a hand or shrugging the shoulders, are language symbols that serve the same function as words. And just like words, they can be used to represent our ideas, feelings, needs and desires.

The significant contribution of non-verbal symbols becomes more evident when we look at children who are born deaf. Many of these children may never learn to speak words. However, their lack of speech does not mean that they do not use language. Many deaf children communicate through a system of non-verbal signs and gestures, such as British Sign Language (BSL), that has all the characteristics of vocal language except that it is not spoken. Instead, BSL is expressed through signs – gestural symbols that represent things in the world the same way words do. Deaf babies, like hearing babies, piece together a language puzzle. The only piece of the puzzle they may not acquire is the speech piece. Still, their language puzzle picture is complete because they are able to substitute non-verbal symbols for the spoken words of language.

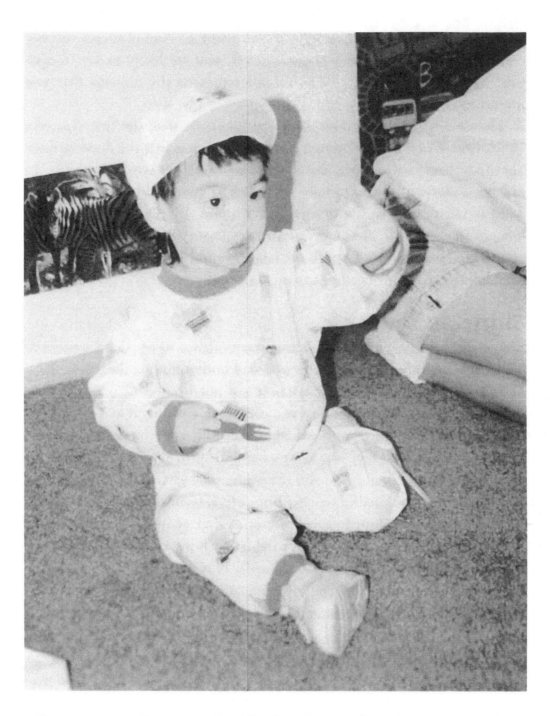

The moon is a salient part of children's books as well as the night-time sky. That's one reason why the palm-twisting gesture, demonstrated here by a fifteen-month-old, has proved to be a popular Baby Sign.

Where Baby Signs Fit In

Just as deaf babies exposed to BSL can use signs and gestures to "talk", so can hearing babies. Fortunately their problem with words is only temporary – but frustrating nevertheless. Fuelled by their intense motivation to communicate but stymied by the complexity of actually saying things, hearing babies welcome the chance to substitute non-verbal symbols temporarily. As we pointed out in Chapter 1, waving bye-bye is an easy gesture that most babies learn to use appropriately before they are able to say the words.

Bear in mind, however, that *bye-bye* is actually one of the easiest words to learn. Many other words are much more difficult for babies to say. For example, what is the likelihood that a twelve-month-old baby will be able to learn the words *elephant* or *kangaroo?* Yet, if they go to the zoo or look at picture books of animals, they are very likely to have developed these concepts and be eager to share their achievement with their favourite people. So why not help them along by suggesting a non-verbal symbol? A finger to the nose or bouncing of the body are both behaviours that most babies, by the end of their first year, can easily master.

So, while we tend to think of language as speech, we need to keep in mind that words are not the only form of language symbols. Baby Signs represent a useful alternative to help children "talk" before they can talk. As such, they help children develop in many other ways as well, including speeding up their completion of the *whole* language puzzle.

The Baby Sign Advantage

When little Jennifer from Chapter 1 brought a book over to her dad and began naming animals with Baby Signs, she was providing clear evidence that important pieces of the language puzzle were already in place. Her father learned a lot about his daughter during that interaction. He learned that she had developed a warm *social relationship* with him that made her eager to find a way to communicate. He learned she was capable of *intentional communication* as a means to give and receive information. He learned she had done the hard work of developing *concepts* of the individual animals – identifying what makes one a zebra and another a hippo. And he learned that she had a clear understanding of what *symbols* are all about. Without the Baby Signs to signal all this, her dad might have appreciated that she could point to things when asked and that she liked to cuddle – but that's about it.

What about Jennifer? We mustn't overlook the fact that the interaction taught her important lessons too. Jennifer's successful use of the signs made it clear to her that she was *right* about a lot of the things she had suspected. She was right that the animals in the book did belong to the categories she thought ("That *was* a hippo!"), that symbols do function to get this information across, that naming things does make Dad smile, and that reading books is a great way to learn more about the things you are interested in. At the same time, her dad's enthusiastic response was providing her with more food for thought. His conversation provided models of how words should be said, whole sentences for her to practise her comprehension skills on, new concepts to add to her list, and the knowledge that he thought she was pretty wonderful. In short, that one interaction was a gold mine for *both* father and daughter. Of course, the same gains would have resulted had Jennifer used the words *elephant* and *hippo*. It's just that it would have been a shame to wait until she could.

Given the many little boosts that Baby Signs provide, it's not surprising that the signing babies in our studies have developed intellectually at a faster rate than the non-signing babies. For example, by the time the two groups of babies were two years old, the signers could not only use their Baby Signs as labels, but also on average knew about fifty more real words than their non-signing peers. Moreover, these gains did not disappear as time went on. A year later at age three, the signers were both saying and understanding words at levels almost comparable to what is expected at age four! They also scored impressively on tests of mental development, fantasy play and the ability to remember where things are.

These babies were definitely tuned in to their environment, both real and imagined. And your baby can be, too. Isn't it about time we got you started?

CHAPTER THREE

Getting Started with Baby Signs

"When I first heard about Baby Signs, I thought, 'But I know nothing about sign language.' Much to my surprise and pleasure, the more I learned about it, the more I realised that I was practically doing it already without even knowing it. It comes so easily!"

– Mother of sixteen-month-old Anthony

Once parents in our workshops learn about the important ways in which Baby Signs can help their babies, they are eager to get started. This chapter describes when to get started, which signs to start with, and how often to use signs.

When to Get Started

Start introducing Baby Signs as soon as your baby begins to show an interest in communicating about things she sees. This typically happens at around nine to ten months but may be somewhat earlier or later for your own child. As with many other aspects of development, babies are not all the same in terms of their interest in communicating, and you are by far the best judge of readiness. A good time to start watching for changes is at about seven to eight months. As soon as your baby seems to want to "talk" about things, it is time to start providing her with some Baby Signs to help her along.

How will you know that your baby wants to talk? One of the most striking signs is an increased interest in people and things around her and connections between the two. She will begin to point to things more than she has before, and her pointing may be accompanied by "Uh, uh!" as if asking, "What's that?" For example, when you go to the park, you may find that she points to the slide, the swing, or a baby in a pram. And, if you are like most parents, you will happily provide the name for each. Besides pointing to things, your baby is likely to show her interest in toys and other objects by bringing them to you and holding them out for you to see, again as if requesting a label. These encounters are all good indications that your baby is interested in "talking" to you about the world and that she is ready to begin Baby Signs.

A second change in behaviour that you may notice around this age is an increased interest in picture books. Instead of focusing on tearing the pages out, babies begin to focus their attention on looking at the pictures on each page. Parents typically respond to this new interest in books by pointing to various pictures and asking, "What's that?" They then provide the label themselves, knowing that their baby is not yet capable of producing the answer. Babies also demonstrate their new interest by pointing to pictures that they find attractive. Their pointing is often accompanied by a quizzical look and eye contact as if they are asking for a name for the object. Observe your baby closely, and your baby's behaviour will tell you when it is time to start using some simple signs.

What if your baby is already using words? Is it too late? If your baby is older than nine or ten months or has already begun to use some words, there are still very good reasons to introduce him to Baby Signs. Our research shows that babies can benefit from Baby Signs any time during their first two-and-a-half years. Remember that a baby's early vocabulary typically consists of a few simple words and that new words are added very slowly. Words like *crocodile, giraffe* and *swing* are difficult for babies to say, yet these are things that interest them when on outings at the zoo or the park or when looking at books. They want to "talk" to you about them but can't because the words are too long and complicated. Baby Signs provide a way for your baby to overcome these obstacles and communicate effectively about a wider variety of things than their words alone would allow. So if your baby has already demonstrated his communication readiness, either with or without words, start introducing Baby Signs right now.

Signs to Begin With

Begin by appreciating the "signs" you are already teaching. If you are like most parents, you are using Baby Signs without even knowing it. For example, you may already have taught your baby to wave bye-bye. Most parents do, taking great pleasure in the accomplishment when their pride and joy waves as Grandma leaves. *Bye-bye* is but one conventional sign that we all use to communicate every day. Nodding our heads up and down for *yes* and side to side for *no* are two others. Babies pick up these gestures too, even though parents are not consciously teaching them. Some parents say, "Shhh", and put their finger across their lips to tell their baby that someone is sleeping. Many babies do the same when they, too, want to comment that someone is sleeping, whether it is Daddy, the pet dog, or someone on TV. Pay attention to behaviours like these that you do automatically, and appreciate your baby's accomplishment when she uses them to communicate with you. Because babies have been seeing these signs since birth, they are often among the earliest Baby Signs learned.

Introduce five "beginners" that are surefire winners. Over the years we have taught our own children to use Baby Signs, and we have helped many other families get started too. Based on our research, we are convinced that the signs for *hat, bird, flower, fish* and *more* are among the easiest and most useful for babies to learn. Therefore, as a way to help you get the feel of using signs along with your words, we suggest starting your Baby Sign effort with these "beginner" signs:

1. *Hat* – Pat the top of your head with your hand open and your palm down.
2. *Bird* – Flap one or both arms out to the side like a bird's wings.
3. *Flower* – Make a sniffing gesture with a wrinkled nose as if smelling a flower.
4. *Fish* – Open and close your lips, smacking like a fish does.
5. *More* – Tap the forefinger of one hand into the opposite palm.

Keep in mind that these signs are just suggestions. The goal of Baby Signs is not to teach your baby a set of specific signs. Rather, it is to enrich the relationship between you and your baby and to provide your baby with the sense of connection that comes with the ability to communicate with others. Also, feel free to modify the form of these signs in any way you like.

If your baby is already saying one or more of these words, then there is no need to use the sign. Instead, pick a substitute that will add something new to the list of things your baby can talk about. For example, if your baby is already saying "kitty", which is easy for some babies to say, then choose another sign to work on. Here are some good substitutes:

1. *Duck* – Keeping your fingers straight, open and close them like a quacking duck.
2. *Cat* – Stroke the back of your hand with your fingers to represent stroking a cat.
3. *Dog* – Open your mouth and breathe shallowly in a panting fashion like a panting dog.
4. *Bottle/Drink* – Put your thumb to your lips and tilt your head as if drinking.
5. *All gone* – Move your open hand, palm down, back and forth in front of your chest.

If these don't appeal to you or your baby, feel free to browse through the suggestions in Chapter 9, or simply create signs on your own. You are the best judge of what will work for you and your baby.

A hat is something that covers your head. This is one concept that fourteen-month-old Leanne had down pat and would "talk" about, pardon the expression, at the drop of a hat.

The bird feeder in the garden was a great place for bird-watching. Here, eighteen-month-old Brandon uses his Baby Sign for "bird" (arms flapping) to tell his mum that the sparrows are back.

Fortunately for us all, the world is full of flowers — in gardens, on wallpaper, in books, on clothes. That's one reason babies tend to catch on to the flower sign so quickly: they get plenty of practice. Here, ten-month-old Bryce clearly demonstrates the appropriate sniffing gesture.

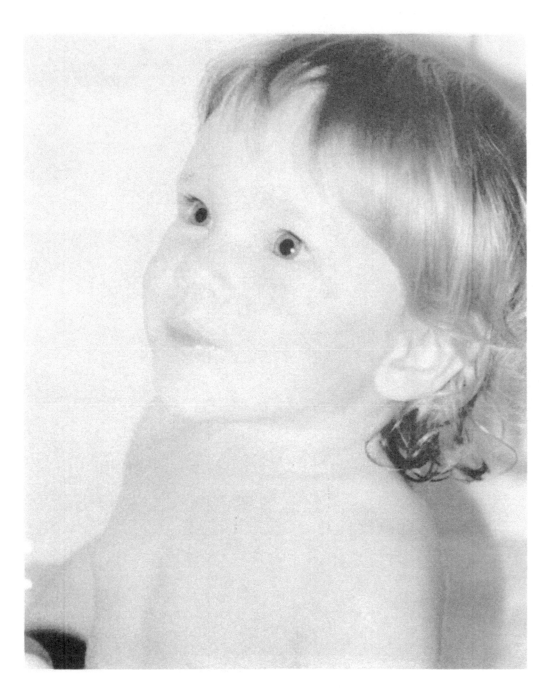

The lip-smacking Baby Sign for "fish", demonstrated here, is particularly easy for babies to learn. One reason may be that it's a variation on a motion they already know well – kissing. Here, bathtime is the occasion for "talking" about a plastic fish.

The Baby Sign for "more" makes a great beginner sign because it is both useful and easy to do. Here, thirteen-month-old Emma uses her version (two fists tapped together) at the nursery to ask for more biscuits.

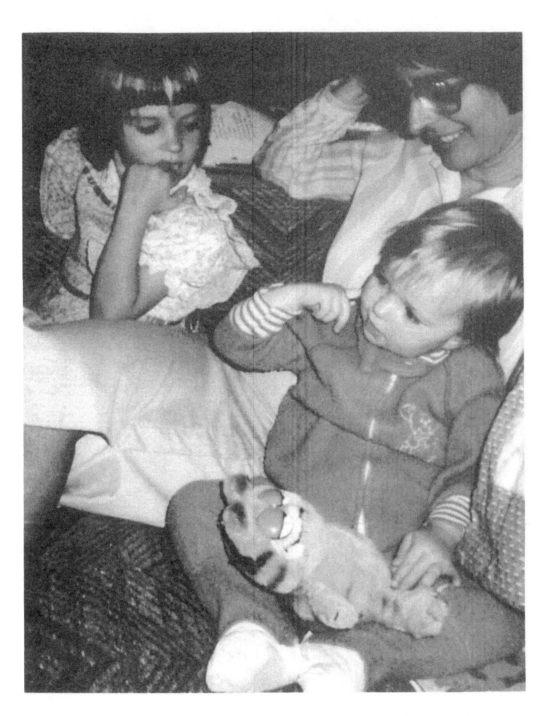

Several different Baby Signs for "cat" have worked out well. Here, thirteen-month-old Carolyn demonstrates a whisker gesture while holding her stuffed cat.

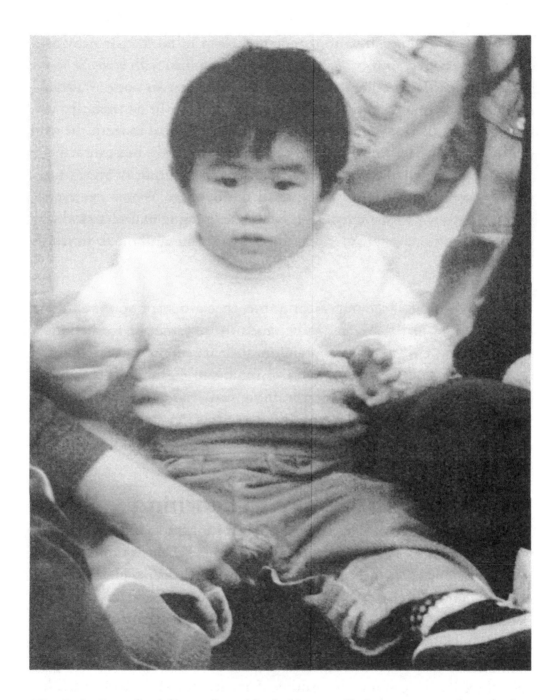

The Baby Sign for "all gone" enables babies to tell their parents when they've finished food, when objects have disappeared, and even when bath water has gone down the drain. The action, demonstrated here (palms flat, back and forth), can be done with one or both hands.

Always use the sign and word together. Keep in mind that Baby Signs are a way to help your baby "talk" by providing him with a *choice*. When he both hears the word and sees the sign he has two options available instead of only one. Some words, like *ball* or *up*, will be easier for your baby to say than others. In those cases, he may choose to learn the word right from the beginning. Other words, like *flower*, may be more difficult, and your baby may therefore choose the sign. By using Baby Signs and words together, you are leaving both doors open. What's more, even when your baby uses the sign first, he will be learning to understand what you are saying and will have a head start in working out how to say the word himself.

Use lots of praise, encouragement and enthusiasm. For your baby to take advantage of Baby Signs, she needs to be rewarded for her efforts along the way. Children love praise from their parents and respond well to words of encouragement. A broad smile and a gleeful "That's right!" go a long way towards making learning fun. Reward early efforts and your baby will soon be using Baby Signs to join you in your conversations. The more enthusiastic you are about Baby Signs, the more enthusiastic your baby will be.

Repetition Is the Key to Learning

The more a baby sees a sign, the easier it is for him to learn it. The best way to remember to use signs frequently is to build them into your daily routines: nappy changing, mealtimes, bathtime, bedtime. Hang a picture of a dog above the changing table and talk about the "doggy," using both the word and the sign, each time you change your baby's nappy. Choose a special book about dogs for your child's bedtime routine. Use a table mat with birds and a bib decorated with flowers as reminders to teach your baby these Baby Signs at each mealtime. Put a fish toy in the bath and fish magnets on the fridge. Try fish-shaped biscuits as a snack, and when they have gone, ask your baby if he wants "more". These are all good ways to ensure that your baby gets lots of exposure to the signs you are trying to teach him. Take advantage of whatever toys and pictures you have on hand, and look for ways to incorporate these into enjoyable, easily repeated routines.

In addition to home routines, look for opportunities to use Baby Signs on family outings. Label birds at the park, flowers on your neighbourhood stroll, toy dogs in the high street, and goldfish in the aquarium at the doctor's surgery. You'll be surprised at how frequently you are using signs and how easily Baby Signs become a part of your daily routines.

Emphasise a sign by repeating it several times. When adults talk to babies, their conversations are typically characterised by repetition. For example, when you point to a bird flying up into a tree, you are likely to repeat the word several times: "Oh, there's a birdie! See the little birdie? See the birdie up in the tree?" Such repetition helps babies identify exactly which word is the important one, the one that needs to be remembered. Do the same with Baby Signs. In these situations use the sign for bird each time you use the word. Soon your baby will appreciate the special connection between the sign, the word and the object. She will be on her way to understanding that things in the world have names that can be used to talk about them. Just as with words, you'll find such repetition comes quite naturally.

Use each Baby Sign with lots of different examples. If you use the sign for *dog* whenever you and your baby encounter any type of dog, he will learn that the sign stands for *all* dogs – real dogs, toy dogs, pictures of dogs – not just the family pet. Use the sign for *more* to ask your baby if he wants more cereal or more juice, or if he would like to read a book over again. Use the sign for *all gone* when he has finished his bottle, when aeroplanes fly out of sight, and even when the bath water is "all gone" down the drain.

Repeating a sign each time you encounter a different example of the same object teaches your baby that, just as with words, Baby Signs can refer to any member of a category. Before long he will begin to work out exactly what features the members of a category share. In other words, he will have developed a concept of that object. Such concepts, whether they deal with dogs versus cats, hot versus cold, or up versus down, are the building blocks of a baby's intelligence. By focusing a baby's attention on the things in the world around him, Baby Signs speed this process along.

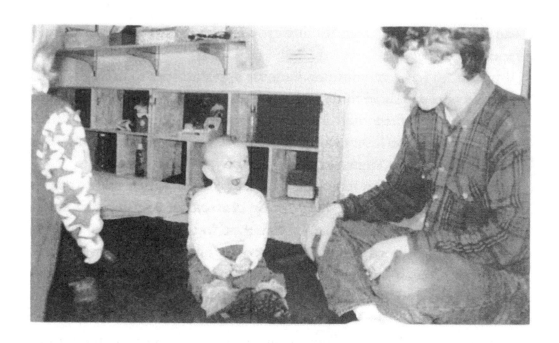

Nyssa's dad is one of her most enthusiastic Baby Sign teachers. Notice in the picture above how carefully she looks at his face, and he at hers, as he models and she imitates the Baby Sign for "frog". Below, we catch them in the midst of a teaching session. In this case she is intent on watching his hands while he demonstrates a Baby Sign for "in".

Watching for Your Baby's Progress

Recognise early signs of progress. There are a number of ways to tell that your baby is catching on to this new language. One of the first things you may notice is that your baby begins to pay more attention to your non-verbal behaviours. We can both recall how fascinated our own children were when, in the early stages of teaching them Baby Signs, we wrinkled up our noses and repeatedly "sniffed" as we pointed to flowers in the garden. Your baby, too, will find your signing quite intriguing and will begin to watch you in anticipation of a new "word". You may even find that she will bring a toy or book to you, then look at your hands as if asking for a sign. These behaviours show she is beginning to understand that these signs are important for connecting with you. As an indication of early progress, watch how your baby watches you.

In addition, watch for evidence that your baby understands the meaning of your signs. Just as babies understand more words than they can say, they also comprehend Baby Signs before they use them. For example, if your baby looks towards the dog when you use the *dog* sign or brings you the toy fish from the bath when you smack your lips, these behaviours show that he understands what the signs mean.

Of course, the most important evidence of progress is your baby's first attempts to imitate your signs. The excitement parents feel when their babies begin to use Baby Signs to "talk" about things is indescribable. Watch for any effort your baby makes to produce a sign, no matter how awkward these first tries may be, and respond enthusiastically. Keep in mind that babies' first words are commonly awkward imitations of adult words. For example, even though an adult says "ball", a baby is likely to say "ba". The same is true for Baby Signs.

Take Dillon and his family's experience with *duck* as an example. As we had suggested, his parents were making their hands "quack" by opening and closing one hand, thumb to fingertips. Even though they always kept their fingers straight, Dillon curved his, essentially opening and closing his fist. His gesture worked well because his parents understood it. They recognised that even awkward attempts are indications of real progress and deserve praise. And what if Dillon had never progressed all the way to the adult version? That would have been just fine too. Keep in mind that the goal is communication, not perfection.

Every parent wants to know how long it takes a baby to show the evidence of progress just described. Days? Weeks? Months? We have seen cases where each one of these was true – and for very good reasons. The speed with which a baby catches on to Baby Signs will depend on lots of things: her age, the number of times she sees the sign, whether or not she's "into" Baby Signs already, her interest in that object, and even whether she'd rather be doing something other than communicating for a while – like climbing the bookshelves. The important thing to remember is to make Baby Signs such a natural part of your conversations with her that the signs will be there when *she* needs them to be.

Differences Among Babies

Expect your baby's age to make a difference. Your baby's age when you begin using Baby Signs is clearly a factor in determining how long it will take your baby to catch on. Generally speaking, the younger your baby, the *longer* it will take him to learn his first signs. To understand why this is so, think back to the first time you held out a rattle for your baby to grasp. If he was *very* young – say, two or three months old – his eyes crossed as he tried to focus on it, his hands flailed out in front of him, and his legs kicked for no good reason at all. Meanwhile the rattle stayed in your hand. But if, instead, he was five or six months old when the rattle first came along, he probably fumbled a bit and then quickly mastered the grasping motion.

Few parents are surprised that it takes time for very young babies to learn a complicated business like grasping objects. After all, lots of skills come together in this one act. The same is true for learning Baby Signs. The younger the baby, the harder it is to pull together the memory, motor and attention skills necessary to learn those first few signs. That's why older babies often catch on to Baby Signs more quickly than younger babies. But no matter what age your baby is when she achieves this first-sign milestone, once the first few signs are learned, she will clearly be on her way.

Given that your baby is likely to learn more quickly if you begin later, you might be thinking, "Why not just wait?" One reason not to wait is simply that it would be a shame to waste the many opportunities to communicate with your baby that Baby Signs would allow in those intervening months. But something else would be lost too. Remember, our research shows that the Baby Signs experience actually *helps* your baby learn how to talk. Words must be heard – and heard many times – before they can be learned. We have consistently found that as parents begin teaching their babies signs, they find themselves *talking* to them more than ever – naming things, asking questions, searching for opportunities to sign. All this talking translates into lots and lots of examples of how to say things with words. In fact, we often describe Baby Sign babies as "bathed in words". Even though a baby may choose to use signs at first, he hears the words and begins to store away memories of how they sound. A little bit later, when his mouth catches up with his mind, these memories are available to help him say the words himself. So begin signs as soon as you see evidence that your baby is ready.

Remember that each baby is unique. Sometimes it is impossible to pinpoint exactly why babies respond to Baby Signs at a different pace. All we can say is they just do. Consider, for example, the experiences of Samantha and Robin. Both little girls were twelve months old when their parents began to use Baby Signs. Extremely energetic, Samantha was already showing an interest in sharing things with those around her, a good sign of readiness. Sure enough, Samantha caught on within two weeks, surprising her mother with a sniff for *flower* when they were out in the garden. From then on there was no stopping her. Over the next two months she added over twenty other signs and quite a few words. Given such an impressive "vocabulary", Samantha was one of the most "talkative" fourteen-month-olds we've ever met!

Robin's experience was different but equally successful. At twelve months, Robin was a cheerful little girl, content to play with toys but also ready to greet almost anyone with a broad smile and uplifted arms.

Robin's mum began Baby Signs at this point and was unusually enthusiastic and creative in finding opportunities to use them. But unlike Samantha, Robin took two months rather than two weeks before she produced her first sign. The occasion was at Christmas dinner, and the motivation was the flower centrepiece on the table. As the family gathered round the table and Robin was put into her high chair, she spied the colourful flower arrangement. Without a moment's hesitation, she looked to her mum, wrinkled up her nose, and "sniffed" away. Robin's mum described to us the look on Robin's face that showed her that the light bulb had come on. Robin proceeded to add fifteen other signs to her repertoire in the space of three weeks. And she didn't stop there. She eventually added an additional thirty-five signs before words burst forth in a gush at eighteen months. Robin's mother had clearly been rewarded for her patience.

There's simply no way to know why these two babies caught on at different times. Children are unique, and many factors play a role in the pace at which babies begin to use Baby Signs. Our best advice is to watch for the behaviours described earlier that indicate readiness, introduce the "beginner" signs, and use them patiently and consistently. In doing so, you will be providing your baby with interesting food for thought, no matter how long it takes him to produce signs himself. Whether your baby is more like Samantha or more like Robin, we know that you will find Baby Signs fun and rewarding from the very beginning.

CHAPTER FOUR

Moving Beyond the Beginner Signs

O nce your baby has caught on to Baby Signs and is watching, understanding or using at least some of the "beginner" signs, start introducing four or five signs of your own choosing. As your baby begins to show evidence of progress, introduce a few more. At the point when your baby is actually using half a dozen or so, feel free to add as many as you feel comfortable with. Remember, the goal of Baby Signs is to enrich your relationship with your child by fostering communication and simplifying daily life. It is not a race that can be won or lost. As with any aspect of learning, it is better to crawl before you walk. Start off slowly, be sensitive to your baby's pace, and you will both be off and running before you know it.

Choosing New Signs

What signs should you add to your baby's growing "vocabulary"? Work out what your baby seems most interested in – what *she* would like to "talk" about. If she really likes Barney, playing with balls or the swing in the park, signs for these things are bound to please her. What foods does

Like many of her contemporaries, Leanne was totally smitten with Barney. Her mother took advantage of her fascination and taught her this hugging Baby Sign. Leanne used it both to label Barney and to request her Barney videos.

she especially like? What are her favourite toys? Which animals does she seem to be particularly interested in when you go to the zoo or when you are looking at books? Are there things around your house that might be interesting or important to communicate about?

One family of a fourteen-month-old boy lived on a farm. Every day Cody would see his father driving a tractor and was clearly fascinated. Because the tractor was such a significant thing in Cody's life, his parents began to use a steering motion as a sign for tractor. Each day when he saw his father returning from the fields, he proudly used his Baby Sign. "That's right, here comes the tractor!" his mother would respond with pleasure.

Another family taught their fourteen-month-old daughter, Anya, a sign for computer – spreading and wiggling all her fingers. With two teachers as parents, Anya was no stranger to the little grey box with the green screen and noisy keys. She loved to see the letters appear and disappear and would beg to be lifted onto the chair to type on her own. She picked up the sign immediately and soon was able to ask for permission to type, a great improvement over the irritating whine she had been using before. The computer was important to her because it was important to her parents, and being able to "talk" about it was both helpful and fun.

Work out what signs would help you as well as your baby. Anya's ability to ask for permission to type on the computer was certainly a boon to Anya, but there's no doubt it was equally important to her parents. No matter where in the house they were, Anya could make it clear that it was the computer she wanted. Before Baby Signs, Anya's parents were frustrated that she so clearly had things to say but no way to say them. Particularly trying were those times when Anya wanted or needed something but simply couldn't get her message across. "Uh uh!" can mean almost anything from "I'm hungry" to "There's a scary dog over there!" One of the most important ways that Baby Signs help parents – or anyone who cares for a baby – is by providing signs for typical, everyday needs. A baby who can ask for cereal when she is hungry, her

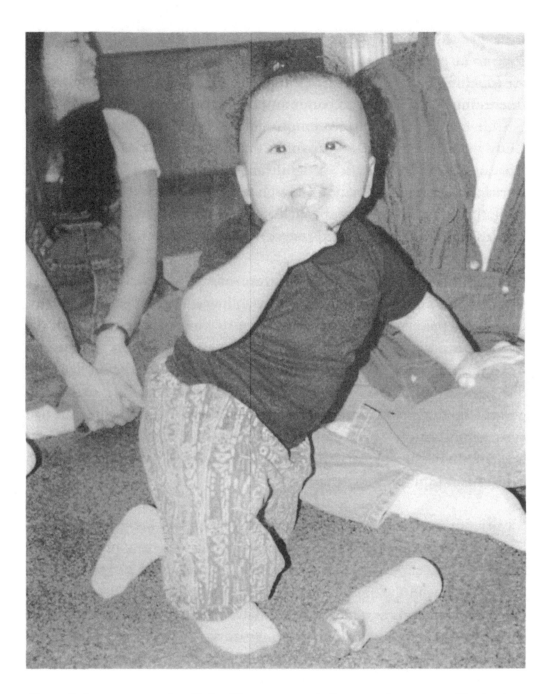

One of the most popular Baby Signs among infants and parents alike is the sign for "bottle" or "drink". Here, twelve-month-old Jasmine uses a typical form of the sign to call attention to the fact that her bottle has just fallen on the floor.

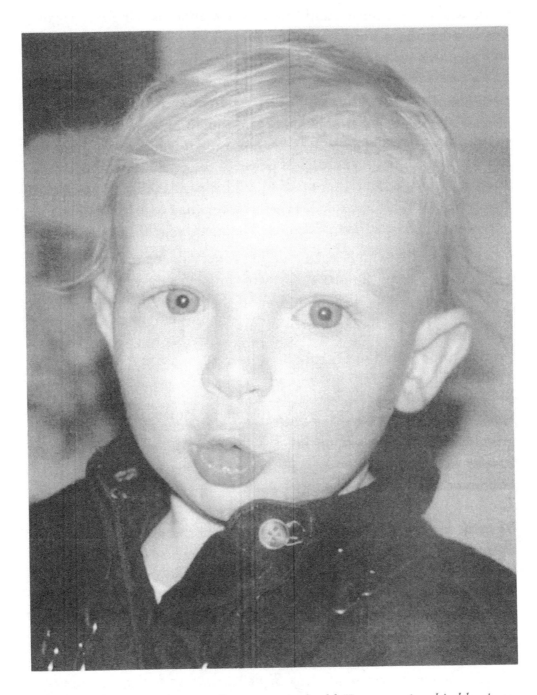

"Boy, is that hot!" comments fourteen-month-old Keegan, using his blowing gesture to let everyone know what he has learned from getting too close to the fireplace.

bottle when she is thirsty, and "more" when either is "all gone" is going to be a much easier baby to get on with.

Parents value other signs because they help keep a baby safe. For example, twelve-month-old Keegan's parents, concerned about his attraction to their fireplace and barbecue, taught him a sign for *hot*. They decided on a blowing motion and began using it regularly with the word hot whenever Keegan approached either of these. He caught on quickly and began to use the sign himself to tell his parents that he knew these things were hot. He also told his parents when food or bath water was too hot, saving everyone time and tears. The usefulness of the sign became especially apparent one day at the swimming pool. As his mother headed towards the water with Keegan toddling at her side, he suddenly stopped and began blowing furiously. Knowing immediately what the trouble must be, Keegan's mother swept him off the hot pavement and up into her arms. Had he simply started crying when his feet began to burn, precious time would surely have been lost.

Other signs that help ward off danger include *gentle* for fragile items or unpredictable pets, *ouch* for sharp objects like pins or broken glass, and *rubbish* or *dirty* for all the *grubby* treasures toddlers inevitably find at ground level. Baby Signs, in other words, are for more than labelling flowers and birds. They can also help you teach your baby some important safety lessons about the world.

Be open to your baby's creations. Once your baby realises that you pay attention to her gestures, she may find opportunities to create signs on her own. In fact, all babies try to use gestures to communicate, even those whose parents have never heard of Baby Signs. The problem is that most parents are so focused on speech that they never even notice. The result is frustration on both sides.

After becoming aware of Baby Signs, parents of Jessica, age twelve months, recalled how she would look at them and pat her chest each night when they sat down at the dinner table. They had no idea why Jessica was doing this and felt helpless as she became increasingly upset.

Once alerted to Baby Signs, they worked out what she wanted: a napkin! With her parents tuned in to her "word", dinnertime became a delight. Jessica clearly and confidently "asked" for her napkin, and her parents happily fulfilled her request.

Spontaneous creations such as Jessica's are common among babies. Pay close attention to your baby's non-verbal behaviours. She may be trying to teach you something.

Choose easy motions. If the word you choose to represent with a Baby Sign is among those in the next chapter, you can simply follow the suggested gestures there. Otherwise, think of gestures that your baby will be able to imitate easily. Hugging your arms across your chest to represent Barney's loving nature, bouncing your hand up and down to depict the motion of a ball, and rocking your hand, palm open, in an abbreviated swinging motion are gestures that most babies can imitate. Pay attention to physical behaviours your baby can already do, and take advantage of these for creating new signs. Keep in mind that you can always modify a sign if you decide the specific gesture you have chosen is difficult or awkward for your baby.

One family modified the sign for *cat* to make it easier for their son, Jeremy, to do. They started by wiping the fingertips of both hands across both cheeks from nose to ear, depicting a cat's whiskers. They soon realised that Jeremy was having difficulty co-ordinating the movement, so they changed it to one finger across one cheek. Very quickly he began to imitate the sign and was soon seeing *cats* everywhere – around the neighbourhood, on TV, in books, and even on the cat food tin at the supermarket.

Making Learning Easy

When it seems helpful, besides simply showing your baby a sign, you can gently manipulate his hands to help him get the feel of the motion. You may know from your own experience how useful it is for an expert to help you form your hands around a golf club or tennis racket as you are

This Baby Sign for "bee" or "insect" requires a very simple motion that babies can easily mimic: the thumb and index finger tapping together. With this sign at her disposal, fourteen-month-old Emily became a superb insect" detector. She used it for all tiny moving things, from ants to mosquitoes.

learning. You quickly get a sense of how the club or racket should feel in your hands, making it easier next time to do it on your own. Babies are no different. In fact, because they are less experienced, they profit even more than we do from sensitively given help. But keep in mind that babies can also be pretty independent at times. Some babies like help, and others prefer to do it on their own. Just pay close attention to your baby's response to make sure he likes your help. As is true whatever the situation, awareness of your own baby's preferences is most important.

Take advantage of books. Reading picture books provides lots of opportunities to use Baby Signs. Babies love going through picture books with their parents, looking to their parents to tell them what is on each page. You'll quickly discover that such books provide a rich source of new Baby Sign ideas. ABC books, for example, typically have pictures of common objects for each letter, many of which can have sign "names" too: A for Anteater (tongue in and out), B for Butterfly (thumbs intertwined, fingers spread and waving), C for Cat (stroking gesture) and so on. But don't feel that you need to think of a sign for every letter. Just be open to the opportunity books present to introduce signs you may not have tried yet.

Simple story books, like Margaret Wise Brown's *Goodnight Moon*, with all its pictures of the moon and the mouse, or Dr. Seuss's *Cat in the Hat*, with all its cats and hats, also are fun to enhance with signs. Babies love reading them over and over again, making it easy to work in lots of practice with the signs you have chosen. Watch for specific things your baby likes as you turn the pages of whatever picture books you have. Try out some signs, and delight in the opportunity Baby Signs give you to generate a two-way interaction. The more your baby sees you using Baby Signs with her favourite books, the sooner she will learn that she too can "talk" about the dog or cat or bird on the page.

Songs and games are fun ways to teach signs. Try teaching your baby a sign for *spider* (rubbing your index fingers together) while singing "The Eency Weency Spider". Then use your new *spider* sign to label lots of

Fifteen-month-old Emma and her mum enjoy a picture book together. As is typical of babies who know Baby Signs, Emma is able to tell her mother about the butterfly she sees on the page.

spiders – real ones, rubber ones and pictures. The goal is to provide your baby with many opportunities to learn that rubbing two index fingers together means spider. Or make up little poems and games to introduce signs. Here's one we use:

> *Crocodile, crocodile nips your nose –*
> *Crocodile, crocodile nips your toes –*
> *Crocodile, crocodile swims around –*
> *Crocodile, crocodile lies right down.*

Using a sign for *crocodile* (your two hands opening and closing together to depict the crocodile's mouth), nip at your baby's nose, nip at his toes, swim your hands (palms pressed together) from side to side, and finally tuck your hands under your chin in a sleeping gesture.

Poems and games such as these are enjoyable and easily repeated. Most of all, they make learning fun. To help you along, we have suggested some poems that lend themselves well to Baby Signs. Look for these in Chapter 10.

Make Baby Signing a family affair! Baby Signs enrich family interactions and so encourage others to get involved. Older brothers and sisters love to help teach the baby new signs, and sitting down to read their baby sister or brother a book is more fun with Baby Signs. The parents in one family asked their six-year-old daughter to draw and colour in lots of pictures of the things her baby brother was learning signs for – flowers, monkeys, fish, turtles and birds. Her creations were then stuck to the fridge, taped to doors and windows, and even pinned to her sweatshirt. She took great pleasure in pointing to them and modelling the signs for her baby brother. And you can imagine the pride she felt when he began to use the signs himself. Given the difficulty many parents have in helping older children accept a new baby, the opportunity Baby Signs provide for brothers and sisters to join the team is definitely a plus.

Grandparents also enjoy being included as a part of the team and love showing off their smart grandchild who can "talk" before she can talk.

Some of the best Baby Sign teachers are older brothers and sisters. Here, four-year-old Brandon models the "book" Baby Sign for his sister, Leanne. From the look of it, his efforts have paid off!

Once they know that Baby Signs actually make learning to talk *easier* rather than harder, they become enthusiastic. And it's no secret that grandparents take particular joy in playing games and teaching songs, both wonderful sources of signs. Riding "horsie" on Grandpa's leg or playing the "So Big!" game with Grandma are among many a child's fondest memories, and being able to request these games using Baby Signs lends added pleasure.

Finally, if your baby is in a nursery or has regular baby-sitters, feel free to tell them about Baby Signs and invite them to join you in teaching your baby. In fact, most carers turn out to be as enthusiastic as parents about Baby Signs. It's not hard to see why. A pre-schooler can talk about what he needs, but an infant or toddler can only hope that someone will interpret his non-verbal signals. Baby Signs increase the chance that this will happen, thus easing the baby's transition from home to nursery. After all, don't we all feel safer in environments where others understand us? Why should babies be any different? We also find that as parents and carers share stories about a baby's progress with Baby Signs, co-operation and mutual respect increase. In short, everyone wins.

CHAPTER FIVE

Off and Running with Baby Signs

"It suddenly seemed like a light bulb went on in her head and she began picking up one sign after another. She'd just watch my hands or face – or whatever. And then we noticed she was even combining them into little sentences! An aeroplane or something would disappear, and she'd tell me, "Aeroplane [arms out] all gone [palm down, back and forth]." It was great!"

– Mother of fifteen-month-old Laney

Babies, like the rest of us, take great joy in newly discovered pleasures, whether those pleasures are toys, tastes or talents. Take learning to walk as an example. Somewhere between nine and fifteen months, babies develop the physical ability to balance on their legs and launch themselves on a seemingly drunken path through space. What a trip! – both literally and figuratively. There's simply no doubt that babies revel in this newfound skill, seeing potential destinations everywhere, from the delicate crystal vase across the room to the strange dog across the park. And so, our formerly bound-to-the-ground sons and daughters are suddenly off and running, while we parents find

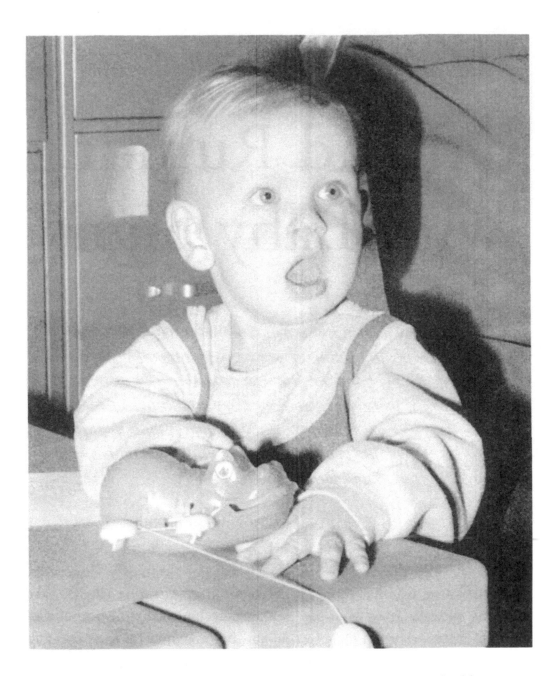

Is that a red plastic hippopotamus on the table? Fourteen-month-old Kai uses a Baby Sign (mouth opened wide) to let us know that's exactly what it is. Kai produced his first sign at twelve months; three weeks later he had twelve in his repertoire. By the time words gushed forth at nineteen months (sixty words in one month!), Kai had learned over forty Baby Signs.

ourselves for the first time following instead of leading our babies around the world.

Something very similar, and equally enchanting, happens as babies catch on to Baby Signs. Just as Laney's mum said in the quote above, it's as though the light bulb goes on. Suddenly the babies seem to understand how this naming game works and take great pleasure in finding things to talk about. "Aha! That's what it's all about! I open my mouth wide, and Mummy knows I saw a hippopotamus!" Suddenly they are true partners in a world of *two-way* communication and are eager to lead the way. Grown-ups are no longer the only ones "talking". Conversations can now start when the *baby* wants them to.

With each new Baby Sign at their disposal, this insight becomes more firmly entrenched. As it does so, babies begin to listen more and more attentively to the words you say and watch more and more closely the things you do. They are eager to get up on their conversational "legs" and set off exploring the world.

Over the years we have watched many babies discover the freedom of expression that Baby Signs allow. As they make this discovery, these babies invariably teach the grown-ups around them an important lesson: the world is, in fact, an amazing place, full of things to see, hear, feel and smell; full of textures, colours and tastes. With Baby Signs to help them, babies find things to talk about that grown-ups didn't even know were there – the caterpillar struggling up the leaf or the pebble that turns pink in the puddle. They grow wide-eyed at the giraffe at the zoo and the goose by the pond. They chase butterflies and frogs and make friends with the wind. And they begin to tell us about it all. As they eagerly explore the nooks and crannies around them, they even more eagerly share with us the exciting news of their adventures. And as they discover things for the first time and share their joy, they give us the gift of rediscovery. This, for many parents, is the greatest thrill of parenting – seeing the world again through the eyes of a child. The beauty of language is that it facilitates this process of sharing. The beauty of Baby Signs is that neither of you need wait for speech for this sharing to begin.

But exactly what kinds of experiences can you expect once your baby is off and running with Baby Signs? That's what we turn to now. Drawing from our own observations of the babies we have studied over the last ten years and the hundreds of stories we've been told by others, we hope to convey some of the creativity and enthusiasm with which babies use Baby Signs.

Here, There and Everywhere

Do you remember how, once you were pregnant, or your wife was, you began to see pregnant women everywhere? Or, having finally decided to buy a particular car, you started to notice how many like it were already on the road? Where did they all come from? Do great minds really think alike? The answer, of course, lies in the heightened awareness that your own situation creates. It's as though you had special radar unconsciously scouting the environment for the things that are momentarily of special importance to you. The same thing happens to your baby when she learns a new sign or new word. With a new label at her command, she suddenly sees examples everywhere – even in places that you, in your naïveté, can't believe they could be.

Take Kai, whose early Baby Signs included a hand-clapping gesture for *crocodile*. His parents modelled it mostly with two picture books and the crocodiles at the zoo. Kai picked it up with enthusiasm at thirteen months and began to see crocodiles everywhere. The most surprising instance was at the shops. With Kai in the buggy, his mum was walking as rapidly as possible from one end of the street to the other, when Kai suddenly squirmed to face her and began to clap his hands, his eyes wide with glee. "What? A crocodile in the street?" But Kai's eager insistence prompted his mum to look around carefully, and to her surprise she found plenty of crocodiles – tiny ones, none more than an inch long, in the upper left-hand front of the men's shirts hanging in the window of the shop they had just passed! "Yes, I can see them! Look at all the crocodiles! Wow, you've got very good eyesight for a thirteen-month-old!" Kai was pleased and proud. His mother had quickly understood and joined him in appreciating his great discovery. She had participated in his world on his

Twelve-month-old Bryce, shown here with his mother, Karen, began using Baby Signs when he was eight months old. As had been true for his older sister, Cady, the sniffing sign for flower was one of his first and one of his favourites.

terms, something that just pointing, even with an insistent "Uh uh uh!" certainly wouldn't have accomplished.

Mothers tell us stories like this all the time. There was fourteen-month-old Eli, whose apple gesture made even a trip to the supermarket a special adventure, what with real apples, apple pies, apple juice and even apple-decorated greetings cards. His mother, like many of us, had never realised how pervasive apples were in the environment until Eli set out to find them all. In a similar way, fifteen-month-old Trina had a love affair with her bird gesture. Everyone expects to see birds through the window or at the park – but at church? Sure enough, embedded in the stained glass windows over the altar were not one, but two, ornamental doves, peace symbols to the congregation but just plain birds to Trina. At least using a Baby Sign was a quiet way to "talk" about them!

Like these parents, you'll find yourself amazed at how vigilant your baby can be. She may only be a baby, but that doesn't mean there isn't lots of mental activity going on behind the scenes. And each time your baby tells you about something with a Baby Sign, she is providing you with a glimpse into all that activity, enabling you to respond appropriately and enthusiastically. In this sense Baby Signs truly are an early window into your baby's mind.

Baby Creations

As we mentioned in Chapter 4, parents aren't the only ones who come up with ideas for signs. Babies create them too. After all, it was Linda's daughter, not Linda herself, who decided to sniff for *flower* and blow for *fish*. Kate was the creative player here, with Linda merely catching up.

In fact, we are convinced that most babies, in their eagerness to communicate, try to use gestures. The problem is that parents rarely notice. Linda eventually noticed because she was a professional baby watcher. But who knows how long Kate had been trying? Maybe she had been about to give up when Linda finally caught on. Fortunately, you need not make the same mistake. Unlike many parents, you will not be so caught up in listening for "words" that you miss your baby's own first Baby Signs.

Being alert to such signs is especially important once your baby is off and running. Your own modelling of Baby Signs is a green light, signalling your openness to this channel of communication. With this realisation, your baby is quite likely to experiment with some of his own. The trick is to know what to look for. Watch for unusual actions that your baby seems to do repeatedly and with a determined air, simple actions linked in time with things around him. Often, but not always, these will be accompanied by a look at you, as if to check to see if you have understood. That was what Jessica's parents, described in Chapter 4, finally noticed. Jessica's patting of her chest and look to them was her attempt to communicate *napkin*, and once they caught on, dinnertime was much more pleasant.

Jessica's choice of patting her chest also provides an interesting lesson in what kinds of gestures babies tend to choose. Our research has shown that babies look to at least two sources for their ideas about signs. First, like Linda's daughter, they often adopt gestures modelled consciously or unconsciously by those around them – like the "Eency Weency Spider" gesture for *spider* and the blowing gesture for *fish*. But babies are also remarkably acute observers of objects on their own. They notice what things look like and what they do, then figure out how to convey both characteristics through gesture, even without you demonstrating. So, for example, Jessica noticed that napkins cover one's chest. Other babies we have studied have noticed, all on their own, that dogs pant, that balls roll, that wind moves things back and forth, that hats cover heads, that fairy lights blink on and off, and that *swings* move back and forth. In each case, the baby spontaneously adapted the characteristic into a Baby Sign. Fortunately for these babies, their parents were smart enough to work out what was going on.

Seventeen-month-old Brandon provides a particularly endearing example of baby creativity. Brandon's parents and grandparents had been modelling Baby Signs since he was nine months old. With their help, he learned *cat, doggy, more* and lots of others that served him well. However, no one had thought to provide him with a sign for one of his favourite objects, the camera. Why *camera*? Brandon was not only a first child, but also a first grandchild. With all the picture taking that had gone on in his short life, there's a good chance he had seen cameras of one kind or

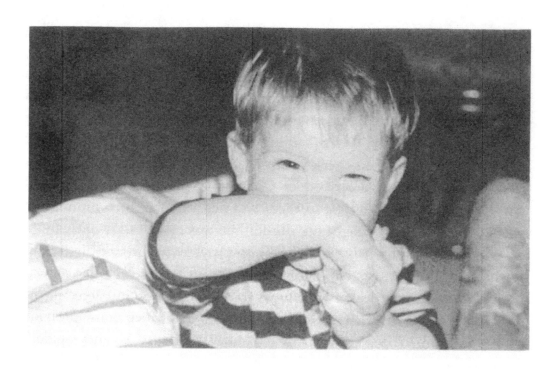

Brandon's fascination with getting his picture taken motivated him to create his own Baby Sign for "camera" (above). No problem deciphering this one! His enthusiasm carried over to helping his little sister Leanne (shown below) learn it too.

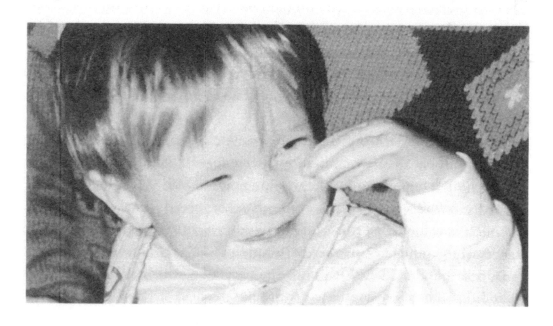

another as frequently as he had his bottle! In fact, by the time he'd reached seventeen months, one had only to lift the camera into place for Brandon to begin to smile and strut about. The camera, in other words, was clearly a significant object in his daily life. So, it shouldn't have been surprising at all when one day Brandon curled his right hand into an arch, lifted it to eye level, and squinted with one eye through the "hole" it formed. It was such an accurate portrait of a camera that there was no mystery about what he wanted. So his mother, Lisa, cheerfully got her camera and snapped a picture of a very proud Brandon grinning from ear to ear.

Like Brandon and Jessica, your baby may surprise you by coming up with a gesture or two on her own. Just be open, observant and enthusiastic. If you do notice such a sign, your supportive response will automatically boost your baby's confidence in her power to communicate and will spur the whole language enterprise. It also, of course, gains you a few early Brownie points with her as a sensitive and insightful parent.

Signs as Metaphors

"His face was an open book."
"My love is like a red, red rose."
"As he slipped on the ice, he was a ballet-dancing hippopotamus, twirling out of control."

One of the most creative ways we use language is to point out similarities between things, similarities that strike us as especially informative, beautiful, or even funny. Such parallels are called metaphors or similes. This kind of creativity represents the poet in us all. You may be surprised, as we were, to learn how early it begins.

As your baby goes on her merry way, picking up information, she inevitably ends up noticing intriguing parallels. And what do babies do when they notice interesting things? Just as with the ladybird on the leaf or the aeroplane in the sky, they are eager to share their discovery. Language allows them to do so, and Baby Signs allow them to do so even

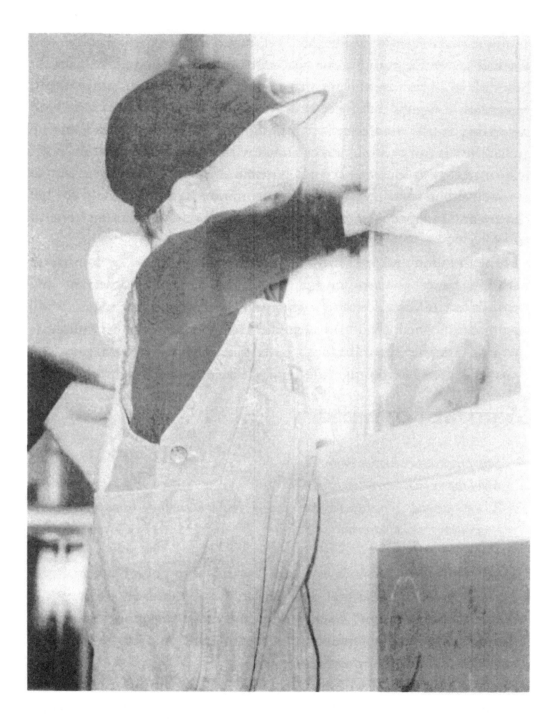

"The Eency Weency Spider" is a good source for several Baby Signs, including this sign for "rain". Here, seventeen-month-old Turner uses the sign to tell us what he sees through the window.

earlier. They simply borrow a Baby Sign from an object the present item resembles, smile expectantly and wait to be congratulated on their remarkable insight. Thus, the earliest form of metaphor is born.

One of our favourite examples of a Baby Sign metaphor was told to us by Sandy, mother of eighteen-month-old Levi. Living in the warm climate of California, Levi had developed as one of his early signs a Baby Sign for the rotating fans so prevalent on ceilings in that area. Levi would lift one hand into the air and rotate it, as though tracing the rotating blades of the fan. One day, the *fan* sign provided just the metaphor Levi needed in order to share his excitement about another object he saw loom large overhead – a helicopter. With its noisy rotating blades, it did indeed resemble a fan, a fan remarkably free of the usual constraint of a ceiling. Levi's pleasure at his own cleverness was clearly evident as he made the gesture and smiled broadly at his mother. "Well done, Levi! That does look like a fan, doesn't it! It's like an aeroplane with a fan on top. It's called a helicopter." Levi's metaphor allowed his mum to do two important things: congratulate Levi on his perceptiveness and provide some new important information that Levi was clearly primed to learn. Once again a Baby Sign had worked its magic.

An evening stroll through the park was the occasion for another Baby Sign metaphor. According to the father of sixteen-month-old Lucy, the family had just come back from a weekend camping trip, where Lucy had been extremely impressed with the stars and the moon. Having lived most of her short life in a city flat, she had never before encountered the majesty of the night-time sky. As Lucy had swung slowly in a hammock nestled in her father's arms, he had leisurely modelled two simple gestures, one for *stars* and one for *moon*. It had just seemed a natural way to keep a sweet moment from ending too soon. As a veteran signer, Lucy caught on right away, almost immediately wiggling her own fingers for *stars* and lifting a rounded hand over her head for *moon*.

It was the following evening back home, however, that occasioned Lucy's metaphor. As they were walking round the small park near their flat, Lucy lifted a rounded hand high over her head and turned expectant eyes towards her father. "The moon, Lucy? But I can't see the moon."

When Lucy repeated the gesture after another hundred yards or so, her father took a second look. This time it was clear what Lucy was proudly pointing out: those old-fashioned, wrought-iron streetlights they had both seen so many times before but had scarcely noticed. With their rounded globes and bright white lights, they did indeed resemble the moon. Her dad's description of this episode conveys one of the indirect benefits of Baby Signs: "It may seem weird to say it, but when Lucy did that, she actually taught me something important. Bring fresh eyes to even an old place, and you may be surprised by what you see."

Other babies have shown similar creativity: eleven-month-old Cady calling the broccoli on her plate a "flower"; eighteen-month-old Elizabeth calling the vacuum cleaner an "elephant"; sixteen-month-old Austin using monkey to describe a particularly hairy young man; and seventeen-month-old Carlos describing a trip through the car wash as "wind" and "rain". Research from many laboratories in addition to ours indicates that the very availability of a label, be it a sign or a word, spurs a baby on to be even more watchful of the things around him. These Baby Sign metaphors show us just how true this is.

Signs in Sentences

"All gone drink."
"Where cat?"
"Big doggy!"
"More biccie!"

                      – Kristen, age fourteen months, ten days

There's no doubt that the single word *more!* uttered by any baby conveys important information. But there's also no denying that the combination *more biccie!* is even better. Babies seem to know this intuitively, and for that reason, every human child eventually does the hard work of learning how to string two symbols together, and the first sentences are born.

Ask any linguist, and he or she will tell you that the appearance of these tiny sentences is a milestone in a baby's life as important as the first word. Although they sound simple enough to us, these two-symbol combinations are thought to signal a quantum leap in the cognitive and memory skills at the baby's command. They also enable the baby to become an even more effective communicator, reducing *everyone's* frustration and adding enormously to the pleasure of social interactions. Clearly, the earlier a baby can make this leap, the better.

When can this remarkable transition be expected? The traditional answer to this question is at about twenty months, with many babies waiting well into their third year. But doesn't that make little Kristen's performance pretty impressive? Here she is, only fourteen months old and already well on her way to conveying more complex messages. How did she do it? Is she unusually gifted? Is she a linguistic genius? The surprising answer is "probably not". In fact, Kristen's performance is one we have come to expect from Baby Sign babies. With an arsenal of signs at their disposal, they simply don't have to wait until they are able to say lots of words in order to start using sentences. The need to communicate is there, the signs are available, and the babies simply "do what comes naturally"; they combine signs with signs or signs with words. Voilà! Sentences!

So little Kristen, highly motivated to get more milk, find the cat, call her mother's attention to the scary dog, and be given another biscuit, formed two-sign sentences to get her messages across. On other occasions she took advantage of the few vocal words she did know, combining these with a Baby Sign or two. By fourteen months Kristen already had at her command the intellectual skills necessary to create sentences. Think about it. This *is a full six months earlier than is typically expected.*

Kristen is not alone. Baby after baby in our studies has charmed his or her parents with little Baby Sign sentences. Babies are clearly much smarter than many give them credit for! What's more, the practice these babies get in combining signs with signs and signs with words actually makes the transition to word combinations that much easier. Consider the following typical sign + sign combinations:

- More + Drink: Many parents have reported this combination. Perhaps the most unusual was twenty-two-month-old Portia, who

The zoo is a great place for animal signs. Here, thirteen-month-old Tristan uses his Baby Sign for "monkey" to tell everyone about the gorilla statue he has just seen. A few months later he was combining signs like this with several others, including "more" and "where"?

used it to tell her mother that the elephant at the zoo was drinking at his trough for a second time.

- All Gone + Water: Twenty-month-old Jennifer loved to stay in the bath to watch the water level go down. As it would finally disappear down the drain, she would use this combination to tell her mother what had just happened.
- Where? + Monkey: Once fifteen-month-old Leanne got used to their size, the gorillas at the zoo were her favourite "monkeys". She frequently used this combination when one of them would retreat into the cave at the rear of the enclosure.
- Dog + Ball: "The dog has the ball" was the message seventeen-month-old Max conveyed to his dad as the family pet ran away with a tennis ball.
- More + Food + Drink: This impressive three-sign combination startled twenty-month-old Sabrina's mum when it occurred one evening at dinner. Obviously Sabrina was still hungry *and* thirsty.
- Where? + Ball + All Gone: Another three-sign combination was used by nineteen-month-old Carlos to ask his mother if she knew where the ball had disappeared.

Babies also frequently combine Baby Signs with vocal words. What is interesting about such combinations from a linguist's standpoint is that they indicate a baby views these two types of symbols as equivalent to each other. To Baby Sign babies, it doesn't matter what kind of symbol is used, only that a message is successfully communicated. The following are just a few of the many sign + word combinations parents have reported:

- More + "Swing": Keesha used this combination at fourteen months to ask to be put back on the swing for another ride.
- All Gone + "Butterfly": Since lots of things in a baby's world disappear, babies often say, "All gone," as well as use the sign for that phrase. This combination was used to explain that a butterfly had flown away.

"Hey, Mum! Where did Mickey Mouse go?" That's essentially fourteen-month-old Kai's question as he plays with a favourite pop-up toy. At first he used this Baby Sign by itself. However, by fifteen months he was combining it with other signs, including "aeroplane", "bird", "dog", "book" and many others.

- Big + "Doctor": It's not unusual for a doctor to look bigger than life to a sixteen-month-old. This is exactly what Dillon was expressing in this particular word + sign combination.
- Hat + "Daddy": As linguists will tell you, the ability to express possession is a major step forward for babies. Andrew, sixteen months old, used this combination when he saw his dad's bicycle helmet lying on the garage floor.
- Water + "Mine": Megan, seventeen months old, was determined to let her playmate know whose water was in the glass on the table.
- "Me" + Eat + Bird: Another three-symbol combination was used by seventeen-month-old Alex to let his mother know that it was his turn to feed the ducks. Note that the *eat* sign is creatively generalised to mean *feed*.

Did you notice that the Baby Signs for *more, all gone* and *where?* seemed to be especially popular in these combinations? There's a very good reason for that. These three signs, like their vocal counterparts, are particularly easy to combine with lots of different items. Everything from buttons to bows can disappear ("all gone"), be hard to find ("where?") and be desired again ("more"). Other signs work in a similar way. Lots of things can be hot or cold, little or big, in or out. Remember this when you are choosing signs to teach your baby. Having a few of these signs in his repertoire will definitely increase the chance he'll be able to use Baby Signs to practise making sentences.

Off and Running – in Different Directions

Once a baby learns how to walk, there's no telling exactly where she will go or what path she will take to get there. Set two babies down in the middle of the park, and while one may head off towards the swings, the other may be content to meander slowly through the dandelions at your feet. Every baby is unique. What is enticing to one may not even be noticed by another. What prompts one to run at full steam might barely inspire another to crawl. In this way the adventure of learning Baby Signs is no different from the adventure of learning to walk. Every baby brings to the Baby Sign experience her own developmental history, her own interest in communication and her own style of interacting with the world. We have seen Baby Signs being used in all the different ways described – to sharpen attention to the world, to focus on similarities, to begin the challenge of producing sentences. However, individual differences reign supreme in this arena as in any other, each baby using signs in a way that suits her best.

CHAPTER SIX

Baby Sign Stories

Over the years of working with families, we have heard many fascinating and heartwarming accounts of ways that babies have used Baby Signs. These stories have been the most fun and exciting aspect of our work. They have renewed our energy when we were exhausted, reinforced our belief in the importance of early communication, and provided us with lots of laughs. But most importantly these stories motivated us to write this book. Parents were constantly reporting how fortunate they felt to have been introduced to Baby Signs. They shared their time, their babies and their stories and encouraged us to share the benefits of Baby Signs with you. It is only fitting that we give these families a voice so that they may share their stories with you too. What follows is a sampling of some of our favourite stories.

"Don't Worry, Mum, I'll Protect You!"

Fourteen-month-old Austin was toddling around the garage while his mum, Jackie, was sorting out baby clothes for a jumble sale. Just as Jackie shifted a large box, a daddy-long-legs scurried out, heading on a collision course with Austin. Austin spied the big gangly insect right away. He looked at it and then to Jackie and signed *spider*. Jackie was just about to say, "That's right, Austin, that is a spider," when Austin, with his trainer-clad foot, stamped heavily on it, squashing it flat. At that moment, Austin looked up at Jackie's surprised faced and, with a big grin of accomplishment, signed *All gone*.

Jackie was amazed at Austin's ability to describe this event with such sophistication. And there was no doubt about it – that "spider" was all gone!

"Read My Nose"

Fifteen-month-old Leannie and her grandmother, Susan, were sitting in the front garden enjoying an ice lolly. Leannie would take a lick and then sign *more* when she was ready for another taste. Susan responded each time with, "You want some more lolly?" to which Leannie would say, "Uh-huh". The routine repeated several times. Once, between licks, Susan picked a flower from the garden close by and handed it to Leannie. The ice-lolly routine continued.

After a couple of minutes, when Leannie signed *more*, Susan, continuing her role, asked, "You want some more lolly?" Leannie replied, "No". Susan, surprised at Leannie's disruption of the routine, said, "You don't want any more lolly?" Leannie signed *more* and then crinkled her nose and sniffed (her Baby Sign for *flower*). "Oh," said Susan, "You want another flower?" A big grin appeared on Leannie's face as she said, "Uh-huh".

As Susan picked the flower, she was once again reminded of the power Baby Signs give to young minds – the ability to express thoughts, feelings and desires before the power of words is fully available.

Sun of My Son

Thirteen-month-old Bryce often had difficulty sleeping through the night. One morning just before dawn he awoke and began to cry. When Bryce's mum, Karen, heard him, she reached over and gave Bryce's dad, Norm, a shake. "It's your turn," she sleepily whispered to Norm. After a few protests, Norm reluctantly crawled out of bed and went in to comfort Bryce, typically not an easy job.

Realising that rocking Bryce was not going to work this time, Norm took Bryce out to the conservatory, sat down in the rocking chair and began to rock backwards and forwards. Norm felt frustrated sitting in the conservatory at 5.30 in the morning when he should have been upstairs in his cosy bed. Settling a bit, Bryce noticed the sun peeping up over the horizon. Still whimpering, he looked at his dad with tear-stained cheeks and signed *light*. Norm's heart melted, and he hugged Bryce tightly. "That's right, Brycie. The sun is coming up and giving us its light." Norm still remembers this as one of his favourite moments with his son.

A Baby Sign Fish Tale

Fish was one of Brandon's favourite Baby Signs. He was quite the "fish detective", searching for fish wherever he went and delighting in "telling" his parents when he found one. His parents' favourite Baby Sign story involved Brandon's first aeroplane trip when he was fifteen months old. As the family settled into their seats, Brandon looked out the window and began to smack his lips enthusiastically, indicating to his parents, Lisa and Jim, that he saw a fish. Lisa and Jim looked out of the window, but it was raining quite hard, and all they could see was water rushing down the outside. They didn't see anything that looked like a fish to them, but Brandon was insistent and continued to look at the window and back to his parents, constantly signing *fish, fish, fish*. It was clear that he wanted them to acknowledge his communication, but for the moment they couldn't work out where he saw a fish.

All of a sudden, the rain on the oval window of the aeroplane looked familiar. In their excitement, Brandon's parents responded at the same time, "Wow! That looks like our aquarium at home. That's right, Brandon. That's where fishies live." A big grin appeared on Brandon's face as he revelled in the glory of his success. Jim and Lisa were amazed at Brandon's keen observation skills and delighted with his ability to communicate so effectively. The other passengers were pretty impressed too!

"Hey, Dad, Can't You 'Hear' Me?"

Keesha, an assertive fifteen-month-old, had finished the rusk her father, Bill, had given her and wanted another. She signed *more*, but Bill was watching a football game on TV and did not respond to her request.

After a couple more polite attempts, Keesha raised her hands up in front of Bill's face and tapped her fingertips into the palm of her hand with great emphasis. Bill told us that it was as if Keesha were shouting, "More, more, more!"

Keesha's mum, Jody, found this very interesting because that very morning was the first time Keesha had shouted in words. Bill and Jody were in the kitchen when they heard Keesha call them, first in her normal voice and then loudly with a shouting intonation "Maaaama, Daaaaadee!" It was another indication to Bill and Jody that Baby Signs and words were one in the same in Keesha's mind.

"Look, Dad, It's a Bird-Horse"

Nineteen-month-old Micah and his dad were window shopping in the high street when Micah spied something that attracted his attention. He became very excited and started signing *bird* and *horse* at the same time. His dad replied, "Oh, you see a birdie?" But Micah shook his head no and continued to used his combined Baby Signs. Then Micah's dad realised what Micah was so interested in: a large mobile dangling from the ceiling in one of the shops. The mobile consisted of brightly coloured winged unicorns flying around and around. Micah had created a Baby Sign compound word – no small feat for a nineteen-month-old!

Robin, the Helmet Patroller

Mark and Ellen live in a university town in which the majority of the population rides bicycles. With the bike helmet law strictly enforced, helmets hanging on parked bikes along the street are a common sight. In fact, Ellen and Mark's eighteen-month-old daughter, Robin, a seasoned Baby Signer, let them know just how typical she thought such a sight was. Ellen, Mark and Robin were strolling back home from a visit to the ice-cream shop when, seemingly concerned, Robin suddenly ran over to a parked bike. She looked all around the bike and then up to Ellen and Mark, who were both wondering what Robin was so concerned about.

Because Robin had a relatively large repertoire of Baby Signs at her disposal and had begun to use these in combination to express more complex concepts, she was quickly able to explain. She patted her head and then raised her hands, palms up, out to her sides and shrugged. Ellen and Mark quickly recognized Robin's Baby Signs for *hat* and *where is it?* Robin persisted, repeating her signs and looking from her parents to the bike in a clearly communicative style. It didn't take long for Ellen to figure out that Robin was asking, "Where is the bike 'hat'?"

Ellen and Mark were so excited about Robin's ability to use her Baby Signs in such a creative way that they called us as soon as they got home to share their Baby Sign story.

"Hey, Take It Easy"

Kathleen, head of a nursery, has been using Baby Signs for several years as a way to facilitate communication with the many infants who have been in her care. One story she told us was how Baby Signs came to the rescue one day for twenty-month-old Tosha. While changing Tosha's nappy, Kathleen lifted her legs, holding her ankles in order to keep her legs high. Tosha said something that sounded like "tie." Kathleen answered, "Tosha, you're saying something to me, but I don't understand what it is. Can you show me what you want?" Tosha raised her hands towards Kathleen's face and stroked the back of one hand with the fingertips of her other hand – her Baby Sign for *gentle* – and repeated, "tie". "Oh, Tosha," said Kathleen, "I must be holding your ankles too tight! I'm sorry. I need to be more gentle."

According to Kathleen, interactions such as this demonstrate just how helpful Baby Signs are in a nursery setting and are exactly why she makes Baby Signs an integral part of her infant care. She introduces Baby Signs both to the carers who work with her and to the families she serves, and she highly recommends that other people who look after infants do the same.

Sleeping Sooty

Zachary, who was totally intrigued with dogs, began to use a panting gesture as a Baby Sign for *doggy* when he was only eleven months old. He used it several times a day to "talk" about real dogs, pictures of dogs, dogs on TV – in fact, anything that looked like a dog. By the time he was thirteen months old, he was even "talking" about dogs when he simply heard barking outside. Zachary would put his hand to his ear (his Baby Sign for *noise*), look to his parents, and then sign *doggy*. Over the next few months Zachary added many more Baby Signs and several words, including *Daddy*, but dogs still reigned supreme in Zachary's mind. He would even use his *noise* sign as a request to go into his parents' room to listen to Sooty, the dog next door (who, unfortunately for Zach's parents, was usually barking).

One night when Zach signed *noise* and *doggy* to his mum, she replied "Do you hear Sooty? Shall we go into the bedroom and listen for her?" Zach enthusiastically nodded. However, once they were in the bedroom, all was quiet. Zach's mum said, "Oh, Sooty must be asleep." Disappointed, but undaunted in his ability to "converse" with his parents, Zach ran back into the living room to share the news with his father. Zach shouted, "Daddy!" and then signed *doggy + sleeping*.

Zachary, at fifteen months, had combined three language symbols! It wasn't until Zach was twenty-three months old that he was able to do the same with words alone. Zach's parents are quick to admit that, had they not introduced Zach to Baby Signs, they would have missed so much of what Zach had to tell them.

Shake It Up, Baby

As we described in an earlier chapter, babies typically create Baby Signs on their own and sometimes use them without their parents' awareness. This was the case with firstborn Megan, who actually introduced her parents to Baby Signs when she was twelve months old. Jack and Carole noticed Megan shaking one fist up and down and clearly looking at them as if she were trying to tell them something. It took a few days, but once they figured it out, they were amazed at how clever Megan was. One night after warming Megan's bottle in the microwave, Carole began to walk towards Megan, shaking the bottle to eliminate any "hot spots". Megan, smiling in anticipation of getting her bottle, began to shake her fist. A light bulb went on in Carole's head – Megan was imitating her mother shaking the bottle. Carole wondered, "Could she have been 'asking' for her bottle these past few days?"

She tested her hypothesis over the next week. Each time Megan shook her fist, Carole responded, "Do you want your bottle?" Sure enough, Megan grinned, nodding her head in affirmation. Carole immediately called her friend Lila, whom she remembered mentioning something about a Baby Sign workshop that Lila and her husband had attended. Through Lila, Carole got in touch with us. We formally introduced Carole and Jack to the world of Baby Signs, and they, along with Megan, became among our most avid supporters!

You've Got a Friend

Kara and Levi, both seventeen months old, are great friends and attend the same nursery. One morning when Levi arrived, Kara watched intently as Levi sobbed at the departure of his parents. After a moment Kara turned to her mum, Joyce, pointed to Levi, then clustered her fingers beneath her eyes in her Baby Sign for *sad*. Joyce responded, "Yes, Kara, Levi is feeling sad this morning." Kara, demonstrating concern for Levi, walked over to him and smacked her lips.

Fortunately, Laura, the carer, saw Kara and knew straight away what Kara was doing. Whenever a baby had difficulty separating from his or her parents, the carers would employ a fish-feeding routine as a distracter. Walking over to Levi, Laura acknowledged Kara's concern. "Hi, Levi," said Laura. "Are you unhappy this morning? Kara thinks feeding the fish might help you feel better." As Laura walked Levi over to the aquarium, Kara followed along, beaming with pride at her own accomplishment. As they have for others who look after infants Baby Signs have become second nature for Laura.

Asleep on the Job

If it's such a beautiful day in the neighbourhood, why is Mr Rogers asleep? Some such thought must have been running through sixteen-month-old Kevin's mind when he ran into the kitchen one day. Mr Rogers was Kevin's TV idol, and hardly a morning went by when he didn't settle down happily to enjoy a mid-morning snack with his favourite TV friend. Kevin's mum, Leigh, had learned to appreciate Mr Rogers, too, not only as a wonderful role model for Kevin, but also as an opportunity to get the morning washing up done. That's why she was up to her elbows in suds when Kevin ran in, tugged at her jeans and made his Baby Sign for *sleep*. "Mr Rogers is asleep?" responded Leigh, somewhat perplexed.

As she paused to consider this possibility, she heard a voice saying, "Well, Mr Rogers, hasn't it been about six months since your last visit?" to which Mr Rogers answered, "Uh-huh." "Well, Kevin," said Leigh, "if Mr Rogers was asleep before, he's certainly awake now. Go and check." But no sooner had Leigh turned back to the sink than Kevin returned, even more insistently signing *Asleep! Asleep! Asleep!* By this point Leigh's own curiosity was raised enough for her to rinse off her soapy hands, grab a towel and follow Kevin back into the living room.

One glance at the TV solved the mystery of how Mr Rogers could manage to answer a question while "asleep". There was Mr. Rogers, lounging in a chair, feet up, head back, mouth open and eyes closed – with Dr Paul the Dentist by his side! From then on, the story of how Mr Rogers fell asleep on the job was a family classic.

Just the Same, Only Different

Scruffy and Dusty, two four-year-old cats, were the prince and princess of the Poulis household. That's probably why a sign for cat was one of the earliest Baby Signs that Rose learned. By the time she was thirteen months old, Rose was routinely letting her family know whenever a cat came along by using her right hand to stroke the back of her left hand, all the way from fingertips to elbow, as if she were stroking a cat. Her mum and dad were pleased at her ability to "talk" about cats and marvelled at her tendency to spot cats a mile away.

However, they were totally unprepared for what they witnessed the day Rose – then fourteen months old – saw her first kitten. As they watched her, fully expecting to see the usual Baby Sign, Rose took them by surprise. Instead of moving her right hand all the way up to her left elbow as she typically did, Rose stopped far short – at the end of her left fingers. She repeated this abbreviated gesture over and over, looking up at them with a huge smile and expectant eyes. With astonishment they realized what Rose was doing: by purposefully abbreviating her normal Baby Sign, she was letting them know this wasn't a full-size cat but just a tiny, little kitten! They had no idea that a fourteen-month-old could be so clever!

Not Just Any Port in a Storm Will Do

There was no doubt about it; fifteen-month-old Emily was upset. Her dad, Ed, had just returned to the sitting room from settling her down for her afternoon nap when the wailing began. Ed was puzzled. He thought he had done everything right. Her tummy was full, her nappy was fresh, she was stripped down to her vest and the music box was playing her favourite lullaby. What could the problem be? As he opened her door, he only needed one look at her face to work it out. There was a teary-eyed Emily, one hand tightly gripping the side of her cot, the fingers of the other hand tapping repeatedly on her lips. Recognizing a Baby Sign, Ed exclaimed, "Oh, Em! I forgot your dummy, didn't I?" With a quick apology, he reached in a drawer, pulled one out and handed it to her.

But Emily frowned and shook her head vigorously. "What's wrong, Em? Don't you want a dummy?" Emily, just as vigorously, nodded her head. At the same time, she stuck out her hands, wrists together and smacked the palms in a clapping motion. Ed immediately recognized the Baby Sign for *alligator*, and the puzzle was solved. "Oh, now I get it!" said Ed. "You don't want just any dummy; you want the one with the alligator on it!" Emily's answering grin told him he was right on the mark.

As he tucked her back into bed, Ed thought to himself that this time he had indeed done everything right – with a little help from Baby Signs.

Stop! In the Name of Love!

The newest addition to twenty-month-old Laney's nursery was a warm-hearted toddler named Marla. From the very first day she appeared, it was clear that Marla loved nursery. She smiled a lot, and that was fine with Laney. She laughed a lot, and that also was fine with Laney. But what was not so fine with Laney was the fact that Marla also hugged a lot. And we're not talking about quick little hugs. Marla was a big girl; when she put her arms around you and squeezed, you *knew* it. After just one or two of these bear hugs, Laney began panicking whenever Marla got close.

The carer, observing all this, knew something had to be done, but what? It took her just a moment to realise that Baby Signs were the answer. Drawing Laney aside, she explained that the next time Marla got too close too fast, Laney could tell her "Stop!" by thrusting her hand out, palm forward. They practised a bit, using a stop-and-go game, and soon Laney was ready to take on the world. It worked! The next time Marla ran over, up came Laney's hand, stopping Marla in her tracks. Then Laney pulled out her trump card. Much to her teacher's surprise, Laney spontaneously followed the stop gesture with a Baby Sign she'd learned at home – *gentle*. Soon all the children were using these two signs, not only to Marla's hugs, but also to other playmates whose actions became a trifle too enthusiastic. As the teacher described it to the parents, Baby Signs had allowed her to introduce "assertiveness training" to the nappy set.

This Little Piggy Went to Market

When Brandon was fifteen months old, he and his family attended the annual street market in a neighbouring town. One of Brandon's favourite attractions was the pot-bellied pig. Because Brandon had a Baby Sign for *pig* (fingertips tapping nose), he was able to "talk" about this intriguing animal. In fact, much to his parents' dismay, he was able to use his sign to ask to see the pig over and over again.

It was a month and a half before the family had a reason to visit that town again. As they were walking along, Brandon began to sign *pig*, in what seemed to his parents a desperate attempt to tell them something. His persistence clearly captured their attention, but as thoroughly as they searched around them, they saw no pigs. Suddenly they realised that they were walking by the spot where they had seen the pot-bellied pig during their previous visit. Once they let him know that they remembered the pig too,

Brandon smiled and stopped signing – his parents had finally caught on.

What Brandon's story demonstrates so clearly is what we have pointed out throughout this book: Baby Signs provide a window into a baby's mind. Through this window, not only were Brandon's parents able to see what he was thinking, they also learned what an incredible memory their son had. Surprises such as these await you, too, as you join the ranks of our Baby Sign families.

As we bring our Baby Sign stories to an end, we'll let seventeen-month-old Turner have the last words: "That's all, folks!"

CHAPTER SEVEN

From Signs to Speech

Anyone who has put together a real jigsaw puzzle has felt the thrill that comes when the end is in sight. Think about it. Doesn't there come a point when so few pieces are left that the pieces seem to float into place by themselves? With so few decisions left to make, the pace quickens. Each piece barely has time to settle before you're sliding a neighbour into place. You're on a roll! In fact, the pull to complete the puzzle is so compelling that nothing short of a major emergency will get you up from the table: "I promise, I'll be there in a minute! (Hmm, this one goes here, that one there, and now just this one, this one, this one, and . . . ta-da! All done!)"

That's very much the way it goes for the jigsaw puzzle of language too. As the pieces fall into place one by one, including the Baby Sign piece, the emerging picture of language becomes so tantalising that your baby is rapidly and irresistibly drawn towards the final piece, conquering more and more of the words themselves. After all, as a veteran user of Baby Signs, he has already learned that communicating is fun, that things have names, and that people like to hear what he has to "say" about them. All that is left is to master the complexities of his vocal cords! ("Hmm, this one goes here, that one there, and now just this one, this one, this one, and . . . ta-da! 'Doggy!'")

Linda holds fourteen-month-old Kai while he uses a Baby Sign to tell her about an aeroplane flying overhead.

You'll notice we've used the phrase *irresistibly drawn* to describe the relationship between your baby and vocal language. The choice is a deliberate one. What we want to convey is the magnetic pull of vocal language for every human child. All over the world, from Tokyo to Borneo, toddlers learn to talk. The final product certainly differs from culture to culture. What stays the same is the use of complex patterns of vocal sounds to convey complex messages from person to person. No culture has ever been found, no matter how isolated from the rest of us, that didn't share this human capacity. Just as all children have two eyes, a four-chamber heart, and hair on the top of their heads, they also all learn a vocal language. Of course, it's true that for a small minority of children, physical, neurological or emotional problems stand in the way. But for all the rest of the world's toddlers, including those who've had the added benefit of Baby Signs, simply nothing will stop them from learning to talk!

But how can we be sure that babies who communicate effectively with Baby Signs won't be so content with them that they lose their motivation to learn words? Don't babies, like the rest of us, believe the old adage "If it ain't broke, don't fix it"? No, they don't – at least not when it comes to communicating with those around them. The reason is simple. As babies grow older their horizons expand and their needs change. And with these changes comes a strong desire for more sophisticated ways of communicating. At the same time, their extensive practice with the other pieces of the language puzzle enables them to develop in the directions they now need. Among other things, they develop the memory capacity, the underlying concepts, the exposure to spoken language, and the neurological maturity required for complex vocal sounds and sentences.

In what ways do babies' needs change? Think about the new places, people, activities and ideas babies encounter after their first year of life. Together, these provide powerful incentives for babies to move towards speech.

New Places to Go

The older your child gets, the less likely she is to stay in one place for long. Where she used to crawl, she now walks. And where she used to

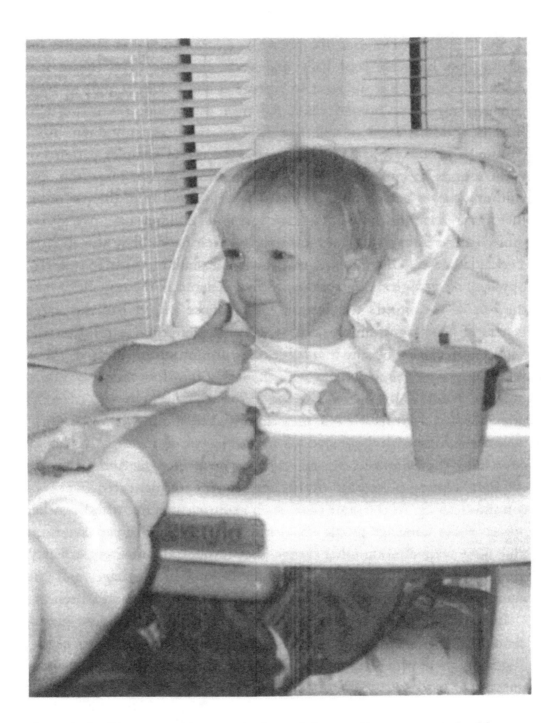

Some Baby Signs resemble gestures that adults use. Fourteen-month-old Keegan shows us one of these as he begins his sign for "drink" (thumb to lips) to tell his mother that he needs a break from the mashed potatoes.

walk, she now runs. Her curiosity takes her round corners, up stairs, into new rooms. At the same time, as a parent, you are becoming increasingly secure that she need not be under your watchful eye absolutely every moment. So your baby enjoys a new freedom to explore the nooks and crannies of her world.

What many of these new places have in common is that your baby can no longer see you, and you can no longer see her. But that doesn't mean she doesn't still want to tell you things. Putting yourself in your infant's place, you can quickly see the problem. As any deaf person can tell you, the usefulness of sign language disappears when people aren't face to face. But sounds, on the other hand! They can be heard – even shouted – from room to room! So, as Baby Signers start to move further and further afield, learning the words behind the signs takes on an urgency not felt when everyone could be counted on to stay in one place.

New Faces to Meet

Greater mobility and maturity also mean that your toddler is destined to meet more and more new people along his way. These may be other families in the park or at the swimming pool, with kids of their own for your child to play with. They may be cashiers or other shoppers at the supermarket, who now talk directly to him rather than just to you. They may be the additional playmates who get added to his nursery group once he's graduated from the infant room. As his circle of friends widens, he will more frequently encounter people who don't understand all his Baby Signs.

Some signs, it's true, will still be understandable because they resemble gestures that adults also use. For example, no matter what your age, the thumb-to-lips gesture continues to signal *drink*, and standing with your hands outstretched and palms up translates into "I don't know" or "Where is it?" But Baby Signs that are unique to your family (e.g., arms up for *Big Bird* or fingers wiped across cheek for *cat*) will inevitably drop out in favour of the symbol system shared more widely – vocal words. All these new communicative partners, then, provide another strong incentive for your growing child to learn the words behind the signs.

New Games to Play

Getting older also means that your toddler will get increasingly skilled at using her body, particularly her hands, to explore and have fun in the world. There are finger paints to spread around, crayons to colour with, puzzles to put together, ladders to climb and trikes to ride. Each of these activities tends to keep hands pretty busy, making Baby Signs less and less convenient to produce. Of course, we still take time out to wave "bye-bye", pretty much regardless of what we're doing. But spoken words gain an edge over signs that they didn't have when your baby was less dependent on her hands for a good time.

New Things to Say

To a fifteen-month-old, simply telling you that he sees a butterfly is a magnificent feat. In such cases a single symbol or two, be they Baby Signs or words, will suffice. However, as children grow intellectually, gathering more and more information about the world around them, the ideas they want to get across become much more complicated. What interests a child at that point is not just the fact that he sees the butterfly, but that this butterfly is like the one he saw yesterday, or that he knows it came from a cocoon, or that its colours remind him of marmalade.

Ideas of this complexity are simply not what Baby Signs are for. Baby Signs are tremendously effective labels for the common objects of the younger baby's world, but by the time a child knows about "yesterday", "cocoons" and "marmalade," it's time to move on. Your child will automatically sense when this time has come and will eagerly conquer the verbal vocabulary he needs.

The Transition Itself

Even though we often get the impression that babies make great intellectual leaps between the time they go to bed at night and the time they get up in the morning, when it comes to the shift from signs to words, the process is usually much more gradual. Once in a while, it's true, we'll see a word appear out of nowhere, and – poof! – the sign is gone. But in the vast majority of cases, the transition proceeds more slowly.

A good example is eighteen-month-old Megan's gradual shift from her *toothbrush* sign (index finger rubbed across her front teeth) to her version of the word ("too-bus"):

1. For about five months, Megan used the sign exclusively, especially when she'd join her mother in the bathroom in the morning.

2. When she was about eighteen months old, Megan occasionally began to mutter something that sounded vaguely like the word, always pairing it with the sign. Her parents had trouble understanding what she was saying and depended on the gesture as a translation.

3. Within about two weeks, the sign and the word were equal partners. Megan used them together pretty consistently.

4. The tables began to turn in favour of the word. Megan still used the sign and word together, but more and more frequently, the word occurred by itself.

5. Megan confidently used the word in all but a few special circumstances (described at the end of the chapter). The transition was complete.

Variations on a Theme

One of the most frequent questions we are asked is, "How soon after a Baby Sign is learned should one expect this transition to begin?" In other words, how long do Baby Signs last? The answer, as usual, is that it all depends. In this case, two factors seem to be especially important: the particular word the Baby Sign stands for and the particular child using it.

The first of these is easy to understand. We've mentioned it before. In general, if the sign is substituting for a relatively easy word like *ball, more* or *cat*, the word is likely to start appearing after a fairly short time. "Short" here can mean anything from two weeks to two months. On the other hand, if the word is long and complicated, like *elephant* or *butterfly*, the sign is likely to stick around for longer. For example, Justin, one of our most prolific signers, replaced his *ball* sign with the word *ball* after only a month. However, his signs for *butterfly*, *alligator* and *dinosaur*, which he learned at fourteen months, continued to work their magic

Emily began using vocal words at a remarkably young age. Does that mean she didn't use Baby Signs? Not at all. She just started even earlier—at eight months. Here is Emily using her Baby Sign for "more" (index finger to palm) to ask for more juice.

until he learned the words at twenty-four months. That's a full ten months!

The second factor, the nature of the child, is both less obvious and more intriguing. As the number of babies using Baby Signs increases, the more apparent it becomes that the signs function in different ways for different babies. Two perspectives seem to be particularly popular. For some babies, signs are seen primarily as a great way to expand the set of things that can be talked about. Their highest priority is to communicate. They are less concerned with which kind of symbol they use than with whether it works to get their message across. In fact, the ability to label something with a Baby Sign seems to free them to expend their energy conquering words for which no obvious gestural symbol is available. If they've got a Baby Sign for *flower* but not for *clown*, they probably will give higher priority to learning the word *clown* than learning the word *flower*. Consequently, these babies tend to hold on to their Baby Signs for a long time, using them to complement their ever-growing verbal repertoires. This is what Justin, described above, had done. In addition to *butterfly*, *alligator* and *dinosaur*, he had kept at least eight other Baby Signs around until twenty-four months, but not because he was generally slow at learning words. On the contrary, by this same age Justin could boast a *vocal* vocabulary of nearly 200 words!

Keesha provides another example of a baby whose primary goal is to use signs to complement her vocal vocabulary. As an avid fan of *Sesame Street*, Keesha eagerly learned a Baby Sign for *Cookie Monster* at fourteen months, keeping it in continuous use all the way to twenty-two months, an impressive length of time. But was this long duration due to an inability to learn verbal names? Far from it. By the time she had reached eighteen months, names clearly were no longer a problem. That's when she learned to say the names of Ernie, Bert, Grover, Oscar the Grouch, and The Count all in one week! Conspicuously absent from this list is Cookie Monster. Why? Since she already had a viable *gestural* name for Cookie Monster, Keesha evidently decided it would be more productive to concentrate her efforts elsewhere.

Using Baby Signs to complement vocal words as Justin and Keesha did

How could anyone resist smiling back at sixteen-month-old Turner as he tells about "Big Bird". His carer, Kathleen, certainly couldn't!

is quite common, but it's not the only option. A second strategy we've seen is the use of Baby Signs to facilitate – and thus speed up – the process of learning the specific words the signs stand for. We first noticed such an approach when ten-month-old Bryce began learning Baby Signs. No sooner would he become skilled at using a sign than the word itself would begin to appear. Sometimes the gap was a week, sometimes two or three, but often considerably shorter than we had come to expect. The pattern didn't hold for every one of Bryce's Baby Signs, but it occurred often enough for his mother to notice and bring it to our attention. She was particularly surprised, she said, because his older sister Cady, a veteran of Baby Signs herself, had *not* tended to use signs in this way. Apparently, even being closely related and sharing the same parents is no guarantee that babies will see eye to eye on how best to learn language!

What's the logic behind Bryce's strategy? How exactly does a sign help a baby learn the word it stands for? We can only guess, of course, but it seems likely that a major factor is the way people respond to Baby Signs. As you will soon find out, it is almost impossible to see a baby do a Baby Sign and not respond by saying the word itself. "Frog! Yes! You're right, that's a frog!" The predictability of such a reaction means that a baby who learns a sign actually has gained considerable control over the number of times she gets to hear the word. The more frequently she uses the sign, the more often the word gets repeated. And the more often the word gets repeated, the more opportunities she has to focus on the sounds that make it up. Once the sound pattern is analysed, it's a much easier jump to saying the word itself.

Some babies seem to have a strong preference for using their Baby Signs in one of these two ways (either to complement the set of words they know or to help them focus on the words they particularly want to learn), but the more typical pattern is for a baby to use signs in both ways. That's another reason why it's really impossible for us to say how long a Baby Sign will last. It all depends.

As you watch your own baby's progress with signs and words, keep these strategies in mind. You'll find it's fun trying to work out why your baby does what he does. Knowledge that these different strategies exist will help you appreciate how much thinking goes on beneath the surface.

Fourteen-month-old Cady (above) is surprised to see her grandmother come into the room with a towel wrapped around her head. Her conclusion? Grandma must have a new hat. Below, Cady, now six years old, looks on as her baby brother, Bryce, uses his swooping-hand gesture to label the cartoon aeroplane they're both enjoying on TV. Cady took great pleasure in helping to teach Bryce a wide variety of Baby Signs.

Babies may not look as if there's method to their madness, but there often is. And once again, you'll have Baby Signs to thank for providing a window into your baby's mind.

Gone but Not Forgotten

Let's jump to the final stage of the transition to speech, the point where the word becomes firmly entrenched. Even after your baby is confidently using the word behind a sign, the chances are that she'll still have the sign available to use in special circumstances. Think about your own use of gestures. Have you completely stopped waving good-bye just because you have the word? No. Like our Baby Sign babies, you automatically recognise occasions when the gesture works *better* than (or better with) the word. The following situations have motivated Baby Signers to revive their signs. It's quite possible you'll find other situations to add to the list.

- **To clarify a message** – Just travel to France without speaking fluent French and you'll get in touch with how valuable gestures like waving can be. Infants face the same dilemma on a daily basis. Learning how to say words clearly enough for adults to understand is a real challenge. A baby may know that "kkk" means *cat*, or "baba" means *bottle*, but that doesn't mean anyone else does. We were surprised and pleased to see how babies with Baby Signs spontaneously use them as clarification when they see a confused look on someone's face. And it works! "Ohhh! 'um-kee' means *monkey*! I see!" Similarly, Megan, described earlier, used a Baby Sign to clarify her word for toothbrush.

- **When food is in the way** – A mouth that's full of food is a real obstacle to intelligible speech. No doubt you can recall times when someone has asked you a question just as you were stuffing a forkful of cake into your mouth. Up come your hands and shoulders, and you shrug "I don't know". The gesture has rescued you from your dilemma. Our Baby Sign babies use their signs in the same way. Max, for example, already had a mouth full of biscuit when his carer at nursery passed by with the biscuit tin. Not willing to let her get away without another portion for himself, Max was able to bypass his mouth altogether by reviving his Baby Sign for *more*. He had been saying the word *more* for several weeks but could still fall back on it when the need arose.

- **For emphasis** – Have you ever said, "Naughty!" while simultaneously shaking your index finger vigorously at your dog or shouted, "Out!" while moving your hand, thumb out, rapidly over your shoulder? There are times, it seems, when words alone simply aren't strong enough. Babies apparently feel this way too. Take twenty-month-old Karen, for example. She had finished her cup of apple juice and was calling to her mother from across the kitchen with the words "Mo dink!" But her mother, busy on the phone, wasn't paying any attention. Karen's solution? She moved right into her mother's face, repeated "Mo dink! Mo dink! Mo dink!" quite loudly, each time pairing it with her old *more* Baby Sign. And she did so with great gusto, hitting her left palm *hard* with her right index finger, as if to say, ". . . and I want it *now*!" Such creativity with gestures seems to come naturally to babies and adults alike.

- **When words can't be heard (or shouldn't be heard)** – Even though words have the advantage of being shoutable, sometimes the noise level is just too high to make even shouting effective. At such times, gesturing comes in particularly handy. We've heard of Baby Sign babies resurrecting old signs for this reason at football games, at circuses and in shopping precincts. The opposite situation, where silence prevails and talking is inappropriate, has also motivated babies to replace words they know with old Baby Signs. James, a twenty-four-month-old with an impressive vocal vocabulary, rediscovered the usefulness of several Baby Signs in church. Another toddler, who frequently visited the university library with her student mother, routinely used her Baby Sign for book even though she'd known the word for months.

Despite their usefulness in these types of situations, there does come a time when Baby Signs truly are forgotten. Ask a four-year-old what he used as a gesture for *hippo*, and the chances are he won't have a clue. Of course, if the Baby Sign is one that is conventionally used by adults, too, such as the shoulder shrug for *I don't know*, the sign will probably escape becoming extinct.

There's one other reason why older children sometimes still know their Baby Signs. Much to our delight, many families have reported that the arrival of a younger brother or sister keeps the older sibling's enthusiasm high. The opportunity to team up with parents to teach the new baby how to communicate is simply hard to resist – especially since Baby Signs are inherently lots of fun for everyone.

CHAPTER EIGHT

Parents' Questions Answered

E ven though you now know what Baby Signs are, how easily they fit into your daily routines, and what benefits they can bring to you and your child, you may still have a number of questions. This is not surprising. In fact, it's quite typical of parents who have attended our workshops and participated in our research studies. Over the years we have found that the questions parents ask at the end of our presentations tend to reflect some common concerns. For that reason, we have devoted a chapter to common questions and their answers. See if any of the questions have occurred to you, too, as you've been thinking about Baby Signs and your own baby.

Q: *I am really excited about using Baby Signs with my son, but he is only three months old. What is the earliest I can start teaching him about Baby Signs?*

A: There is no specific age at which we can say all babies will be ready for Baby Signs. The age at which parents should begin will differ from baby

Cady's parents began modelling Baby Signs when she was just seven months old. They got their reward when she began using them herself a month later. Here, at nine months, Cady uses her sign for "frog" (tongue in and out) to label a toy frog on the table.

to baby. However, there are some general age guidelines that we can suggest based on what we have learned from the Baby Signers in our research studies. Firstly we can tell you that three months is too young. Your son has not yet developed enough of the language puzzle for the Baby Signs piece to fit. We also know that some babies as young as eight months have successfully used Baby Signs. Rather than focus on the age of your baby, it is more important to watch for the behavioural indications of readiness that we discussed in Chapter 3, "Getting Started with Baby Signs."

The age at which you should start with your baby is the age at which he shows interest in communicating about the things around him, sometimes evidenced by his pointing to things. But it is also important to remember that, just as there is no harm in talking to your son before he is ready to talk, using Baby Signs before he is ready will certainly not hurt him if you are willing to be patient. So it's really OK to start when *you* feel ready. Start with just a few signs, and keep in mind that for all babies the first signs take the longest. Should your baby need a little more time to catch on, be prepared to wait – you'll soon be reaping the Baby Sign rewards.

Q: *I taught my baby a sign for "hat", and she has been using it for a couple of weeks now. Do I have to keep using the sign myself, now that she is using it regularly?*

A: No. Once your baby has a particular sign firmly established and is using it regularly, you no longer need to use it too. In fact, you will find yourself quite naturally using a word without its sign once your baby is using the sign fluently. When your baby sees a hat and uses her Baby Sign for *hat*, you can let her know that you understand what she is talking about by saying, "Oh, you see a hat?" The word itself will do perfectly well to let your baby know that you understand what she is talking about.

However, because Baby Signs are so easy to use as well as words, it is certainly OK to continue using a sign long after your baby has been using it routinely. Sometimes doing so can bring unexpected benefits. Several

Here's thirteen-month-old Carolyn demonstrating the easy gesture for "hat" that has proved to be such a popular Baby Sign.

parents have reported that using the signs became so automatic they would find themselves spontaneously combining two or more Baby Signs, unintentionally providing a new learning experience for their child.

At sixteen months Jasmine signed "duck" as she and her father, Peter, went into her bedroom to begin her bedtime routine. Without even realising what he was doing, Peter said and signed "What duck?" (Hands out, palms up for "what"?; fingers to thumb in a quacking motion for "duck".) Jasmine responded with a two-sign combination, "Duck book," to which Peter replied verbally, "Oh, you want to read the book about the ducks tonight?" Only at this point did Peter realise he had used the two Baby Signs without even thinking. More important, he realised that Jasmine, for the first time, had used a simple sentence.

Once your baby has begun to use a sign fluently, you don't need to continue using the sign yourself. But you need not stop either.

Q: *If my baby is able to get what he wants without using words, won't he learn that he doesn't have to talk?*

A: As we stressed in Chapter 7, Baby Signers are pulled towards words by many forces. Of all these incentives, perhaps the most basic is the fact that babies learn language primarily to connect with other people and get their needs met. By using words to label and request things, babies become active partners in communication and forge strong bonds between themselves and others. Far from getting in the way of this process, Baby Signs provide a bridge that makes the transition from no language to full-fledged language.

Baby Sign babies don't sit around helplessly waiting until words are possible. Instead, they are able to plunge right in to the thick of human communication. They begin to learn the social rules of conversation and find out early just how much fun communicating can be. In short, using Baby Signs does not inhibit a child's motivation to talk. On the contrary,

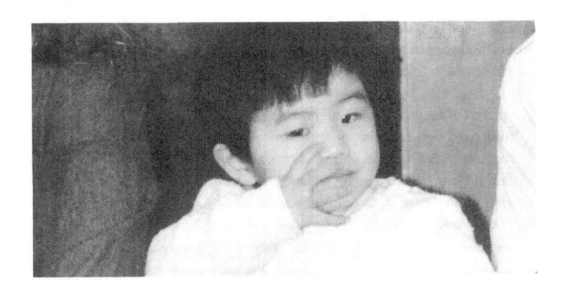

Like first words, Baby Signs often do not take the exact form of the adult versions. The staff at a nursery modelled two fingers to the cheek, depicting cat whiskers for "cat", and two fists under the eyes for "sad". This baby gives "cat" a try, dragging his fingers across his mouth.

A 16-month-old from the same classroom (below) demonstrates his version of "sad" (two fists to his nose) during the "Three Little Kittens" song.

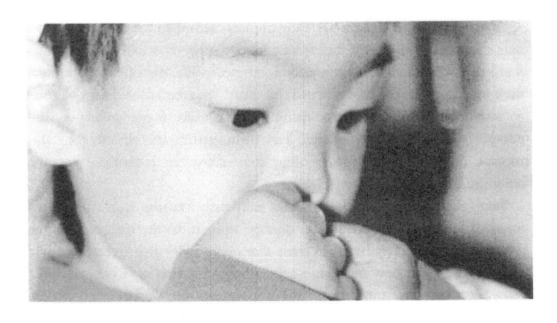

it makes children even more eager to master the words that will enable them to expand their social network.

Q: *If I start using signs, doesn't that mean that I won't be talking to my baby as much?*

A: No. In fact, just the opposite will happen. As we've pointed out in earlier chapters, when you begin to add Baby Signs to your interactions, you will actually talk to your baby *more* than you did before. Remember our description of Baby Sign babies as "bathed in words".

This happens for a number of reasons. Not only are you using words at the same time as the signs as you teach them, but once your baby is a fully-fledged signer, you will also be responding to her own attempts to get conversations started. When she begins to look at you and "sniff" while strolling through the park, you are likely to respond, "Oh, yes, those *are* pretty flowers." When she steps into the bath and begins to blow repeatedly, you will whisk her out and expound on how hot the water is and how sorry you are not to have discovered it yourself.

What these instances have in common is that your baby is calling your attention to things that *she* wants to talk about. This is an exciting change, and like most parents, you will find it impossible to resist continuing the conversation. And when you do respond to her efforts, the information you provide includes many samples of what speech is like and how sentences are formed. Even though your baby may choose to use a sign for a while because a particular word is too hard to say, she is certainly learning what the word sounds like, so that she can more easily use the word herself when she is able.

At the same time you are responding to conversations she initiates, you will also notice yourself looking more enthusiastically for things to talk about. The result, again, is that you provide lots of exposure to her final goal – words and sentences. Once we noticed that the parents in our research studies who taught Baby Signs to their babies also started talking more, it came as no surprise that the Baby Sign babies understood language better than other babies and even developed words faster.

Cereal is a perennial favourite among babies, Emma included. Like other
Baby Signs introduced by her nursery carers, this gesture for "cereal"
(finger and thumb together) helped keep frustration levels low.

Q: *I have been tapping my two index fingers together as a sign for more, and my baby still just taps his two fists together. He doesn't seem to be making any progress towards using his fingers. What should I do?*

A: Many parents have expressed a similar concern. Our advice is to give him lots of praise for what he is doing. Remember that the goal of Baby Signs is to help the two of you understand each other, not to teach your baby a very specific set of motions. In fact, the beauty of Baby Signs is that a sign can consist of any gesture that works.

One mum told us that her son Oshi would rake his fingers across his mouth as a sign for *cat*, even though her form of the sign consisted of wiping two fingers across her cheek as if they were cat whiskers. Oshi's rendition only resembled hers, but that didn't mean she couldn't understand him. This is really no different from what happens with words. Babies' early words often sound quite different from adult words. Babies try their best, but it's not easy to master the complexities of clearly articulating the sounds of language. Despite the crudeness of these attempts, parents still provide lots of praise and encouragement. If a baby says, "goggy", or "nana", parents enthusiastically respond, "That's right, that's a doggy!" or, "Oh, you want a banana?"

If your baby's signs only approximate what you have been showing him, that's OK. Pay close attention to what he is trying to tell you, and let him know that you understand and are thrilled with his effort. It really makes no difference what form his gesture takes. As long as you each know what the other is "saying", Baby Signs are working.

Q: *Both my husband and I work full time, and our daughter goes to a nursery. As we are not with her all day, I assume Baby Signs won't work for us. Right?*

A: Wrong! Like many working parents, you may think you can't take advantage of Baby Signs because you are away from your baby a good part of the day. But remember, you are also *with* your baby a significant portion of her waking hours, especially at weekends. What better way to enrich your time together than to "talk" with one another.

Using Baby Signs takes no extra time. They simply fit into whatever it is you are already doing. For example, Baby Signs work very well during those early-morning dressing and eating routines. And think of the many things you see on your way to the child minder – things you can "talk" about even with one hand on the steering wheel. (You can make this easier by using one of those special mirrors on your dashboard that lets you see your baby in the back seat. Such a mirror not only enables you to monitor your baby's position, but also to appreciate things she is using Baby Signs to point out to you along the way!) And when you are both tired at the end of the day, Baby Signs can be particularly useful. This is a time when frustration most easily arises. By clarifying your baby's needs, Baby Signs help dinnertime, bathtime, and bedtime routines go more smoothly. As a result, these typically hectic times become a lot more fun!

Here's another important point to keep in mind. If your baby spends each day with a child-minder or at a nursery, there's no reason to exclude these carers from your Baby Sign team. Let them know how important you think it is that your daughter is able to "talk" to people she is with on a regular basis. Tell them what Baby Signs are and how Baby Signs will help your daughter to communicate her needs, feelings and interests. Better yet, let them read this book. We have found that most caregivers are as excited about using Baby Signs as parents are. In fact, nursery managers often ask us to present workshops on Baby Signs to staff and parents. These managers recognise that working with Baby Signs makes carers more observant, responsive and appreciative of the small steps that babies take along the way.

Remember, Baby Signs provide a window into your baby's mind that anyone can look through! So let your daughter's carers know which Baby Signs you are using, and keep them abreast of her progress. Encourage them to develop any Baby Signs that fit into their daily routines and then let you know what is happening during the day. Most parents are pleased to find that carers are eager to talk to them about their baby and to be included in something so special. So if you are working parents, give Baby Signs a try. You'll be pleased with the results.

Q: *I'm a single mother, raising my baby on my own. You say it helps to have other people teaching him signs too, but is that absolutely necessary?*

A: As we described earlier, anyone who spends time with your baby on a regular basis can be involved in teaching Baby Signs – friends who visit frequently, baby-sitters, even older neighbourhood children. But remember, as nice as it is to have others involved, Baby Signs need not be a "family affair" to work. Many single parents raising their babies alone have described to us the ways in which Baby Signs have enriched their relationships. Just listen to this single mum:

Jake and I spend quite a bit of time alone, and with a baby so young, that can sometimes feel pretty lonely. That's why from the time he was born I could hardly wait for Jake to begin talking. But after attending the Baby Signs workshop when Jake was ten months old, I realised I didn't have to wait until he could carry on a conversation with words before we could "talk" to each other. I began using Baby Signs with him straight away, and he caught on pretty quickly. Within about three weeks he was using several signs regularly. Lots more followed. It was great to see what pleasure he took in "telling" me about planes, flowers, dogs, and cats and how confident he was when he could let me know whenever he wanted "more" biscuits, cereal, juice or milk.

If you and your baby are the only ones using Baby Signs, that is just fine. In fact, using Baby Signs can help form a special bond between the two of you. When he finds he can "talk" to you and be understood, frustration will be reduced for you both, leaving more time and energy for the positive interactions that bring closeness and joy to any relationship.

To get this photo of sixteen-month-old Brandon using his "hippo" sign, his dad asked him what animal they had seen swimming under the water at the zoo.

Q: *I have been using Baby Signs with my fourteen-month-old son for the past two months, and he is still not showing any evidence of developing any signs or words. My sister's baby is only twelve months old, and already she has learned six Baby Signs and four words. What does this mean about my baby's development?*

A: Nothing except that your son's priorities are different. Remember, babies are unique individuals. They have their own interests, motivations and timetables. In fact, during the course of our research, we commonly found individual differences in the age at which the first Baby Sign and the first word were acquired, as well as the rate at which words and gestures were added.

For example, Aaron began to use both Baby Signs and words before the age of twelve months and developed a large vocabulary of both signs and words over the following year. Aaron's pattern of development was typical of many children who use Baby Signs to supplement their words during the first year.

Carrie's development was quite different from Aaron's. She also began using Baby Signs at a very early age, but she did not produce her first word until fifteen months. However, because she began learning lots of Baby Signs at eleven months and used them frequently, she, like Aaron, was able to "talk" about things that were important to her.

A.J.'s development represents still another pattern of using Baby Signs. A.J. used his first sign when he was about twelve months old. Two days later, he said his first word. Although he continued to learn new Baby Signs and use them to talk about things for which he did not yet have words, it was clear that he was off and running in speech almost from the very beginning. For A.J., Baby Signs merely filled in the gaps until his verbal language skill could completely serve his communication needs.

Hannah's development was characterised by a fourth pattern in which both Baby Signs and words are slower to develop. Like some babies, Hannah seemed more eager to invest her energy in other directions — learning how to use the climbing frame and play hide-and-seek with her

Even babies who aren't interested in learning a huge repertoire of Baby Signs usually include the sign for "more" as one of the chosen few. That's probably because of its connection to one of their favourite pastimes – eating.

brothers. Hannah did not begin to use Baby Signs or words until around fifteen to sixteen months. Even then, when she did begin to "talk", her progress was relatively slow. Over the next two months she developed only about ten words. At the same time, however, she also learned seven Baby Signs. Even though Hannah's verbal vocabulary was somewhat smaller than that of other children her age, her use of Baby Signs almost doubled the number of language symbols she had at her disposal.

The bottom-line lesson we have learned from all these children is that what is important is to be patient and pay attention to your specific baby's preferences and developmental priorities.

Q: *If my baby uses Baby Signs, won't other people have trouble understanding her?*

A: Although it is true that people who do not spend time with your baby may not understand some of her signs, the same is true for every baby's early words. Fledgling attempts that strangers have difficulty understanding are often crystal clear to parents. In such cases, parents automatically assume the role of their baby's interpreter to the rest of the world. If anything, Baby Signs are easier to understand than first words because many of the signs you will use resemble the things they stand for. For example, many families represent *bird* with a sign that looks like a bird flapping its wings. Imagine seeing a baby at the park, looking at some birds and flapping his arms. In a situation like this, it is quite easy to tell what the baby has in mind. Similarly, an expectant look and a fist to the ear when the telephone is ringing are hard to miss as a symbol for *phone*.

The other point to remember is that at these early ages, the significant people in a baby's world are usually relatively few – family members and carers. These are the people that your baby cares about "talking" to. Nine times out of ten, these are the people who will be doing Baby Signs with him.

Q: *My wife and I are not into baby songs and games. Do we have to use these to introduce new signs?*

A: Absolutely not. Even though some parents find it fun to take advantage of songs, poems and games, their use is certainly not necessary for learning to take place. You'll still have many different opportunities to teach your baby about Baby Signs, including book reading, visits to the zoo, mealtimes and bathtimes. In fact, any interaction between you and your baby has the potential for teaching a new Baby Sign. Using signs in everyday situations is not only effective but also very important. It shows your baby that signs are bound not only to songs and games but are also useful for "talking" about lots of things in the real world. Once you begin to use Baby Signs, you will be surprised how easily they fit into your daily routines. Soon you will be using them almost unconsciously.

CHAPTER NINE

Sign Suggestions

The following Baby Signs are some that were used by families with whom we have worked in the past. They were created by parents and babies to help them "talk" about things that were interesting and important in their daily lives.

While these Baby Signs give you lots of possibilities for communicating with your baby, remember that these are only suggestions. Create new ones of your own, and watch your baby for evidence of his or her creations. Also keep in mind that the descriptions for each Baby Sign can be modified in any way that is easier or more enjoyable for all of you. Remember that one reason Baby Signs are so easy is that they are so flexible. There is no right way to use any Baby Sign. Whatever you and your baby choose is right for you.

Object Signs

AEROPLANE
Description:
Arms out stiffly or one hand swooping
Memory Aid:
Depicts the wings or mimics the flying motion of an aeroplane
Possible Situations:
To real aeroplanes and pictures
When talking about an aeroplane trip

BARNEY
Description:
Hugging motion, hands crossed over chest
Memory Aid:
Depicts Barney's loving nature
Possible Situations:
To Barney on TV
To pictures of Barney
Requesting to see Barney

BIB/NAPKIN
Description:
Patting chest
Memory Aid:
Depicts placement of bib or napkin during mealtime
Possible Situations:
To label or request a bib or napkin

BIRD

Description:
Flapping arms out to sides
Memory Aid:
Mimics wings flapping
Possible Situations:
To real birds outside and pictures
To talk about Big Bird

BOOK

Description:
Holding hands flat with palms up, opening and closing
Memory Aid:
Mimics opening and closing book or turning pages
Possible Situations:
To books and magazines
Requesting to read a book
Describing someone reading

BUMBLEBEE/INSECT

Description:
Thumb and forefinger together moving about in air
Memory Aid:
Mimics the movement of flying insects
Possible Situations:
To real flying insects and bees
To pictures in books

BUNNY/RABBIT

Description:
Wrinkling nose or holding two fingers up in a V

Memory Aid:
Mimics bunnies' nose movements or depicts rabbit ears

Possible Situations:
To real rabbits at pet shop or zoo
To pictures, especially at Easter

BUTTERFLY

Description:
Hands together, fingers waving

Memory Aid:
Mimics the flapping movement of butterflies' wings

Possible Situations:
To real butterflies, especially during outings to the park
Watch for pictures in books

CAMERA

Description:
Hand curled in front of eyes

Memory Aid:
Depicting the lens of a camera in front of face

Possible Situations:
To cameras, including videocamera
Request for photograph to be taken

CANDLE/FIRE

Description:
Index finger to mouth with blowing motion

Memory Aid:
Mimics blowing out a candle

Possible Situations:
To real candles or fire
To pictures of a birthday cake
Request to blow out candles

CAR

Description:
Steering motion

Memory Aid:
Mimics driving a car

Possible Situations:
To real or toy cars, lorries, or tractors
To pictures of vehicles
Request to go for a ride

CAT/KITTEN

Description:
Stroking back of hand with other palm or clawing motion

Memory Aid:
Mimics stroking a cat or a cat's clawing

Possible Situations:
To real or toy cats
To pictures in books or on posters

CATERPILLAR/WORM

Description:
Wiggling forefinger

Memory Aid:
Mimics a caterpillar or worm
crawling

Possible Situations:
To real caterpillars or worms
To snakes at the zoo

COMPUTER

Description:
Fingers apart wiggling up and
down

Memory Aid:
Mimics typing motion

Possible Situations:
To things with keyboards:
computers, pianos, typewriters
Request to use the computer or
play the piano

COOKIE MONSTER

Description:
Palm to mouth and eating noise

Memory Aid:
Mimics *Sesame Street's* Cookie
Monster eating cookies

Possible Situations:
To pictures of Cookie Monster
To Cookie Monster on TV
Request to watch *Sesame Street*

CROCODILE

Description:
Hands together at wrists, palms clapping

Memory Aid:
Depicts a crocodile's jaws opening and closing

Possible Situations:
To crocodiles or alligators at the zoo
To toys and pictures in books

DOG

Description:
Tongue out, panting

Memory Aid:
Mimics the panting of a dog

Possible Situations:
To the family pet and other real dogs
To pictures and toys

DUCK

Description:
Fingers to thumb, opening and closing

Memory Aid:
Mimics duck's bill in quacking motion

Possible Situations:
To real ducks in the park
To toys and pictures

ELEPHANT

Description:
Finger or back of hand to nose moving up and down

Memory Aid:
Depicts an elephant's trunk

Possible Situations:
To real elephants at the zoo or circus
To pictures in books

FAN

Description:
Index finger up and circling

Memory Aid:
Mimics the motion of a ceiling fan

Possible Situations:
To real fans in homes or restaurants
To label helicopters

FISH

Description:
Mouth opening and closing

Memory Aid:
Mimics the motion of a fish's mouth opening and closing

Possible Situations:
To real fish in an aquarium
To pictures in books

FLOWER

Description:
Sniffing (at a distance)
Memory Aid:
Mimics smelling motion
Possible Situations:
To flowers in the garden
To floral patterned fabric

FROG

Description:
Tongue in and out
Memory Aid:
Mimics frog catching insect with tongue
Possible Situations:
To Kermit the Frog from
Sesame Street
To pictures in books
To label a frog's croaking

GIRAFFE

Description:
Palm rubbing front of neck
Memory Aid:
Depicts the distinctive long neck of a giraffe
Possible Situations:
To real giraffes at the zoo
To posters or pictures in books

HAT/HELMET

Description:
Tapping head with palm of hand

Memory Aid:
Depicts the placement of a hat or helmet

Possible Situations:
To label someone wearing a hat
To ask to put on a hat

HIPPO

Description:
Mouth open wide, head back

Memory Aid:
Mimics the mouth of a hippo

Possible Situations:
At the zoo and in books

HORSE

Description:
Torso bouncing or one foot tapping floor

Memory Aid:
Mimics horse-riding motion or horse's foot stamping

Possible Situations:
To request to play the "Ride a Little Horsie" game
To real horses, pictures and toys

KANGAROO
Description:
Both hands patting tummy
Memory Aid:
Depicts distinctive pouch of
a kangaroo
Possible Situations:
At the zoo and to pictures in
books

MONKEY
Description:
Scratching armpits
Memory Aid:
Mimics monkey's scratching
motion
Possible Situations:
To real monkeys and pictures
To songs and games about
monkeys

MOON
Description:
Hand high, palm up, circling
motion
Memory Aid:
Depicts the round shape of a full
moon
Possible Situations:
To the moon at night
To round globe lights

NOISE

Description:
Index finger pointing to ear
Memory Aid:
Depicts noise coming into ear
Possible Situations:
To label any noise
To request to hear something
(e.g., music)

RAIN

Description:
Wiggling fingertips moving
downwards
Memory Aid:
Mimics the motion of falling rain
Possible Situations:
To say that it is raining
To label or request a shower

SLEEP

Description:
Palms together to side of cheek
Memory Aid:
Gesture from "Now I Lay Me
Down to Sleep"
Possible Situations:
To describe someone sleeping
To request to go to sleep

SPIDER

Description:
Forefingers rubbed together
Memory Aid:
Motion from "Eency Weency
Spider" song
Possible Situations:
To pictures and real spiders
To "The Eency Weency Spider"
and other rhymes

STARS

Description:
Hand up, fingers spread and
wiggling
Memory Aid:
Represents the twinkling motion
of stars
Possible Situations:
To the stars in the sky
To "Twinkle, Twinkle" song

SWING

Description:
Rocking torso, fists raised
Memory Aid:
Depicts swinging while holding
on
Possible Situations:
To label the swings in the park
To request to swing

TELEPHONE

Description:
Fist to ear

Memory Aid:
Depicts holding receiver to ear

Possible Situations:
To say the phone is ringing
To real and toy phones
To pictures of people talking on the phone

TIGER

Description:
Hands up as claws and clawing down

Memory Aid:
Mimics the clawing motion of a tiger, lion or bear

Possible Situations:
At the zoo or when watching big cats on TV
To pictures in books

TOOTHBRUSH

Description:
Index finger across teeth

Memory Aid:
Mimics motion of brushing teeth

Possible Situations:
To ask to brush teeth
To label toothbrushes

WATER
Description:
Palms rubbing together
Memory Aid:
Mimics washing hands
Possible Situations:
At the duck pond
To pools or the sea
To ask to wash hands

ZEBRA
Description:
Fingers spread, moved across chest
Memory Aid:
Depicts the distinctive stripes of a zebra
Possible Situations:
To real zebras at the zoo
To pictures in books and on posters

Request Signs

Baby Signs help your baby get what he or she wants. For example, when your baby has finished all the cereal in her bowl, she may use a sign to request "more" to eat. The following are some signs that our babies have used to communicate their requests. Try these and create some of your own. Also be aware that any of the object signs described above can be used to request that object. For example, your baby may use the *Kermit* sign to label Kermit when she sees him on TV. But if your baby looks towards the TV when it is not turned on and uses her *Barney* sign, she may be trying to tell you that she would like to watch *Sesame Street*. This is her way of using an object sign to make a specific request.

DRINK/BOTTLE

Description:
Thumb to mouth, tilting up

Memory Aid:
Mimics a drinking motion

Possible Situations:
To request a bottle
To request juice or water

FOOD/EAT

Description:
Fingertips to lips

Memory Aid:
Depicts putting food in mouth

Possible Situations:
To request something to eat
To label food or someone eating

IN

Description:
Fingertips of one hand through circle of other

Memory Aid:
Mimics one thing moving into another

Possible Situations:
Request to go inside
Request to get into the bath

MORE

Description:
Index finger tapping opposite palm

Memory Aid:
Depicts putting something into one's hand

Possible Situations:
Request more food or drink
To ask to do something again (e.g., read another book)

OUT

Description:
Knob-turning motion

Memory Aid:
Mimics opening a door to go out

Possible Situations:
To request to go outside
To comment on people or things outside

UP

Description:
Index finger pointing up

Memory Aid:
Depicts an upwards direction

Possible Situations:
To ask to be picked up
To request to go up (e.g., up the stairs, to the top of the slide)

Other Useful Signs

Baby Signs need not fit into any category to be useful. Remember, anything that helps you and your baby communicate better is a useful sign. You may find that you and your baby like to describe things, so signs like big and little add to your conversations. Or you may develop Baby Signs to express emotions like scared. Don't worry about what type of Baby Sign you are creating. Just be creative and use what works.

ALL GONE
Description:
Palm flat, moving back and forth
Memory Aid:
Depicts an empty space
Possible Situations:
To say that food or drink is all gone
To comment that something has gone out of sight

BIG
Description:
Hands straight up over head
Memory Aid:
Mimics the "How Big Is Baby?" game
Possible Situations:
To describe big things
To label Big Bird

HOT
Description:
Hand out, palm down, retracting
Memory Aid:
Depicts touching something hot
Possible Situations:
To comment on hot food, cooker,
bath water, pavement

SCARED
Description:
Hand tapping chest repeatedly
Memory Aid:
Depicts heart beating fast
Possible Situations:
When frightened of something
To label a scary picture

SMALL/TINY
Description:
Thumb and forefinger together
Memory Aid:
Depicts small or tiny size
Possible Situations:
To describe small things
To request a small amount

WHERE?/I DON'T KNOW

Description:
Palms out at shoulder level and shrug

Memory Aid:
Conventional gesture for "I don't know"

Possible Situations:
To ask where something or someone is
To respond to a question

CHAPTER TEN

Sign Time, Rhyme Time!

Babies love a good rhyme. Just ask Mother Goose! For generations babies have taken pride in learning poems about eggs falling off walls, cows jumping over moons and mice losing their tails. The sillier the better!

Among the most loved of all of these unforgettable characters is that poor little spider who never gives up – you know, the "eency weency" one. Part of that spider's charm, of course, is the fact that babies can act out its story, using simple gestures that stand for all the important parts. Linda's daughter, Kate, made the transition from these to communicative Baby Signs – and so can your baby. With "The Eency Weency Spider" as our inspiration, we've composed two dozen or so new poems, each designed to sneak in a few Baby Signs in a context that both babies and adults will enjoy.

Butterfly wings go fluttering by –

(Butterfly – left to right)

Down to the flowers and up to the sky.

(Butterfly – down, then up)

Butterfly wings tickle your toes –

(Butterfly – to toes)

Butterfly wings land right

on your nose!

(Butterfly – to nose)

The kitty-cat is sleeping;   *(Cat)*

Hear her purr.   *(Cat)*

Softly, softly stroke her fur.   *(Cat)*

[Pant, pant] Said the dog

As he pleaded with the flea.

"I won't scratch you

    (scratching)

If you don't bite me!"

    (thumb to fingers)

Birdie fly fast –   *(Bird – fast)*

Birdie fly slow –   *(Bird – slow)*

Birdie fly high –   *(Bird – high)*

Birdie fly low –   *(Bird – low)*

Birdie fly here –   *(Bird – left)*

Birdie fly there –   *(Bird – right)*

Birdie fly round and round everywhere.

    (Bird – around)

When the stars are out   *(Stars)*

And the moon is bright –   *(Moon)*

Blow out your candle [wfff]

   (Candle)

And say, "Sleep tight."

   (Sleep)

A little girl said to Barney one night,

   (Barney/Hug)

"Where do you go when I turn out the

light?"   *(Where Is It?)*

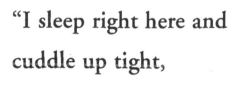

"I sleep right here and

cuddle up tight,

   (Sleep)

And keep you cosy and

safe all night!"

   (Barney/Hug)

My silly little puppy
Came running to my side,
With tongue hanging out
And tail wagging wide.
[Pant, pant, pant] said the puppy –
[Pant, pant, pant] I said, too –
'Cause to little silly
puppies,
[Pant, pant, pant]
means "I love you!"

Bunny ears UP –

(Bunny)

Bunny ears DOWN –

(Bunny – fingers bent)

Bunny ears wiggling
all around.

(Bunny – wiggling)

One last drink of water

(Drink)

My favourite teddy bear –

A lap to curl up in –

(pat lap)

And the old rocking chair

(rocking torso)

A book about kittens   *(Book; Cat)*

A song about love –   *(Hug)*

And I'm off to dreamland   *(Sleep)*

With the stars up above.   *(Stars)*

Barney, Barney,

(Barney/Hug)

Hug me tight!

Barney, Barney,

(Sleep)

Say, "Good night!"

Birdie in the treetop *(Bird)*

Proud and wise –

Here are his wings, *(Bird)*

And here are his eyes. *(point to eyes)*

Down on the ground

A cat he spies. *(Cat)*

UP he jumps,

and off he flies! *(Bird)*

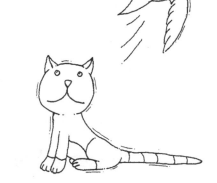

First the boy wants in *(In)*

and the girl wants out *(Out)*

They open the door *(rolling hands)*

and turn about.

Then the boy wants out *(Out)*

and the girl wants in *(In)*

And they end up going

(arms crossed, index

fingers pointing)

to where they have been!

The Hungry Hippo

"Ahhh!" said the Hippo,   *(Hippo)*

  "There's pizza on the breeze!"

    At that he waddled into town

And ordered one with cheese.

"Ahhh," said the Hippo,   *(Hippo)*

Spotting pineapple and peas.

"They're perfect for my pizza!

Please add on two of these."

"Ahhh," said the Hippo   *(Hippo)*

When he heard some chickens sneeze.

"What a tasty topping!

Please add on three of these."

"Ahhh," said the Hippo,   *(Hippo)*

Spying monkeys through the trees.

"They surely would be spicy!

Please add on four of these."

"Ahhh," said the Hippo   *(Hippo)*

When he saw some cows on skis.

"A final splendid topping!
Please add on five of these."
But when he saw his pizza
    (Hippo)
Piled high with cows and peas,
He loudly moaned, "Oh yuck!
Just bring a salad, please!"

When a frog gets hungry,

All he has to do

Is flick his tongue like this:

[flick] (Frog)

And he's got a fly to chew!

When a crocodile gets hungry,

All she has to do

Is snap her jaws like this: *[snap] (Crocodile)*

And she's got a frog to chew!

The Eency Weency Spider

The eency weency spider went up the

   waterspout. *(Spider upward)*

Down came the rain *(Rain)*

and washed the spider out. *(All Gone)*

Out came the sun *(Sun)*

   and dried up all the rain. *(palms upward)*

And the eency weency spider *(Spider upward)*

   went up the spout again.

[*Smack, smack*] **Say the fishes**   *(Fish)*

   as they swim so fast.

[*Smack, smack*] **Says**   *(Fish quietly)*

   the minnow;

[*Smack, Smack*] **says**   *(Fish loudly)*

   the bass!

See the baby on her horse

   (baby bouncing on knee,

   faster and faster)

Bouncing every day.

Faster and faster

She gallops away!

Where oh where has my little cat gone?

(Where Is It?) *(Cat)*

Where oh where can she be? *(Where Is It?)*

With her ears cut short *(hands to ears)*

And her tail cut long, *(hand tracing tail)*

Oh where oh where can she be?

(Where Is It?)

What happens to the stars

At the end of the night, *(Where Is It?)*

When the moon disappears *(Moon)*

And it turns all light?

Do they hide in a closet? *(Where Is It?)*

Do they hide in a drawer? *(Where Is It?)*

Do they find a cosy bed

And sleep forevermore? *(Sleep)*

Little lost duck came

    quacking by.

      (Duck – right hand, right to left)

Little lost duck began to cry.

    (fists to eyes)

Little lost duck heard his

    mummy QUACK.

      (Duck – right hand, right to left)

Little lost duck came running back!

      (Duck – left hand, left to right)

Into the clouds –

    All gone plane –   *(All Gone)*

    Into the tunnel – All gone train

      (All Gone)

    Water in the bath tub

      (Water)

    All gone down the drain!

      (All Gone)

"There's a baby in my
pouch!" *(Kangaroo)*
Said the mother kangaroo.
"He's hiding in there 'cause he's
tiny and new." *(Little)*
"There's a baby in your pouch?"
 (Kangaroo)
Asked the brother kangaroo.
"Can't I jump in and snuggle
 there, too?" *(In)*
"You're much too big!" *(Big)*
Said the mother kangaroo.
"But my lap will always have room
 for you!" *(pat lap)*

Tree high – *(Butterfly high)*
Knee high – *(Butterfly at knee)*
Butterfly, butterfly *(Butterfly across body)*
Fluttering by.

A silly little monkey   *(Monkey)*

Called me on the phone.

(Telephone)

"Hello? Hello?

Are you all alone?

I'm a silly little monkey   *(Monkey)*

Calling from the zoo.   *(Telephone)*

If you're very lonely,

I'll come and visit you!"

Soon that silly little monkey   *(Monkey)*

Was knocking on my door   *(knocking gesture)*

And growing a banana tree

(growing gesture with hands)

Right through my kitchen floor!

The caterpillar said to the bird with a sigh,

"I can only wiggle,   *(Caterpillar)*

but you can fly!"   *(Bird)*

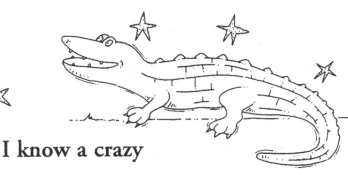

I know a crazy

  crocodile *(Crocodile)*

Who snaps at all the stars. *(Stars)*

He thinks they're sugar sprinkles

On dark blue chocolate bars.

I know a crazy crocodile *(Crocodile)*

Who tries to eat the moon. *(Moon)*

He thinks it's made of marshmallows

That must be eaten soon.

I know a crazy crocodile *(Crocodile)*

Who snaps his jaws at ME!

  (point to self)

He thinks I'm made of

  gingerbread –

And he's quite right, you see!

"More, More, More!"   (More)

Shouted little Tommy Torr.

"Out, Out, Out!"   (Out)

Shouted little Tommy Tout.

"In, In, In!"   (In)

Shouted little Tommy Tin.

And then they began all over again!

   (repeat as desired, faster and faster)

"More, More, More!"   (More)

Shouted little Tommy Torr.

"Out, Out, Out!"   (Out)

Shouted little Tommy Tout.

"In, In, In!"   (In)

Shouted little Tommy Tin.

And then they decided that had to be the
end!

Giraffes are tall –   (Giraffe)

Birdies are small –   (Bird)

But little baby fleas you can't
   see at all!   (tickle baby or self)

Further Readings in Infant Sign Language

For those interested in reading more about the background research in Infant Sign Language (academically known as "symbolic gesturing"), the following articles are recommended:

Acredolo, L. P., and Goodwyn, S. (1985). Symbolic gesturing in language development: A case study. *Human Development*, 28, 40–49.

Acredolo, L. P. (1988). Symbolic Gesturing in Normal Infants. *Child Development*, 59, 450–466.

Acredolo, L. P., and Goodwyn, S. W. (1990). Sign Language among hearing infants: The spontaneous development of symbolic gestures. In V. Volterra and C. Erting (eds.), *From gesture to language in hearing and deaf children*. New York: Springer-Verlag.

Acredolo, L. P., and Goodwyn, S. W. (1990). Sign Language in Babies: The significance of symbolic gesturing for understanding language development. In R. Vasta (ed.), *Annals of Child Development* (vol 7, pp. 1–42). London: Jessica Kingsley Publishers.

Goodwyn, S. W. and Acredolo, L. P. (1993). Symbolic gesture versus word: Is there a modality advantage for onset of symbol use? *Child Development*, 64, 688–701.

Index